SCRAPS
Judy Martin

CROSLEY-GRIFFITH PUBLISHING COMPANY, INC.
Grinnell, Iowa

Dedicated to Steve, Kate and Will Bennett
and all of the quilters, twitters, grouters, and trucklers of the world (my computer
spell checking program's suggested substitutions for a carelessly typed "quilters")

Acknowledgments
All designs are Judy Martin originals.
I appreciate the contributions of the follow-
ing people who made quilts to supplement
my own: Ardis Winters, Margy Sieck, Linda
Medhus, Chris Hulin, and Sherry Folks. I also
appreciate the talented machine quilters whose
work graces my quilts: Nichole Webb, Linda
V. Taylor, Margy Sieck, Kathy Olson, Sherry
Rogers-Harrison, Renae Haddadin, Linda
Mae Diny, and Pam Clarke.

Special thanks to Steve Bennett, Chris Hulin,
and Margy Sieck for proofreading this book
so carefully.

ISBN 0-929589-11-4
Crosley-Griffith Publishing Company, Inc.
P.O. Box 512, Grinnell, IA 50112
(641) 236-4854
toll free in U.S. (800) 642-5615
web site: http://www.judymartin.com
e-mail: info@judymartin.com

Photography by Dean Tanner
Primary Image, Des Moines, IA

Printed in U.S.A. by Acme Printing

Contents

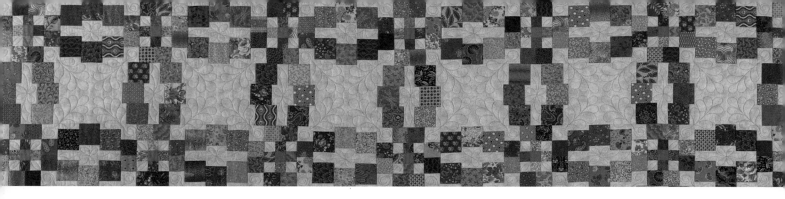

Introduction to Scraps

For me, even more than the pattern or colors, the scraps make the quilt.

Without scraps, a quilt lacks a certain *je ne sais quoi*. Perhaps scraps are an indication that the maker put her heart into the quilt. Perhaps scraps provide the uniqueness that distinguishes a quilt from a mere blanket. Perhaps scraps simply make the quilt more beautiful. Whatever it is about scraps, it is something I want in my quilts and something worth talking about.

My first quilt was a scrap quilt. In fact, it was a box of scraps that started me

on this 36-year (and counting) quiltmaking odyssey. I had come home from college for Thanksgiving break, but home wasn't there anymore. My parents had divorced and moved into houses that bore little resemblance to what I had left behind just three months earlier. I no longer had a bedroom—or even my own bed. While I was searching through the stored remnants of my former life, I came across a box of sewing scraps. I think I was looking for some thread of continuity in my life, and here it was. The wrap-around skirt from eighth grade, a favorite dress, enough shirts with Peter Pan collars to outfit the Lost Boys: all were represented in colorful bits of fabric.

I determined to make a scrap quilt that very weekend.

(And I had everyone sidling along the edges of the living room while my quilt patches occupied most of the floor.) Long story short: I don't believe the divorce left me scarred; the new house eventually became home; and that first quiltmaking experience changed my life.

They may not change *your* life, but it is clear that

scrap quilts certainly can tug at the heartstrings.

Even if it was made from fabrics purchased for the sole purpose of making quilts, a scrap quilt has extra emotional content based simply on its resemblance to that icon of family history, your grandmother's (or even somebody else's grandmother's) scrap quilt.

Years ago, when I sold my patchwork at crafts fairs, I was struck by how many people stopped to look at my quilts and fondly recall a mother or grandmother who had made quilts. Even though it wasn't *their* sisters' school dresses or *their* mothers' patient stitches in my quilts,

something in those scrap quilts spoke of family and love.

I ran out of those old scraps after my first couple of quilts. (And I wasn't generating any new scraps as quiltmaking had pre-empted all of my other sewing activities.) In those days of double knits (another reason for the demise of my dressmaking), woven cottons were not easy to come by. You had to buy it when you found it (or so I convinced myself). Before long, I had a little stash going, and by the time I moved eight years later, the volume of my stash exceeded that of all my other earthly possessions put together.

Scrap quilts today are seldom made from cutting remnants or salvaged pieces from old clothes.

Rather, they are made from fabrics collected for the purpose of making quilts. Even long ago, some quilters doubtless took pains to assemble the desired mix of colors for their scrap quilts.

Today's scrap quilt may not evoke memories of Auntie Em in her apron or Sis in her school dress. Nevertheless, it invokes images of Mom in her sewing room surrounded by fabric she has collected with care to reflect her own sensibilities.

Fabrics purchased on trips or received as gifts take on added significance for the maker.

This perky blue piece with strawberries brings to mind the little quilt shop I frequented in Oregon in the early '70s. That gold 19th Century reproduction reminds me of a vacation with Steve and the kids when we stopped in Old Sturbridge Village. There's the blue print Steve bought me when we learned we were expecting our son. And the lilac and aqua the children so proudly presented to me for Christmas when they were barely school age. There are the pieces given to me by a particularly enjoyable batch of students at a retreat. And the many fabrics I have purchased at quilt shops I have visited on road trips all over the country with my quilting buddies.

Every scrap holds memories for me.

Even without this connection, I would be drawn to scrap quilts. They are, quite simply, more interesting than other quilts: more interesting to look at and more interesting to make.

Nothing else says "quilt" quite like a scrap quilt.

What do scraps do? They make some parts of the quilt stand out more than others. This can be a subtle effect, where areas of stronger contrast or brighter colors whisper, "I'm unique." Or the effect may be profound, where a patch shouts out, "Look at me!" In any case,

scraps add depth and nuance to a quilt.

Nobody makes a quilt for want of a blanket anymore. After all, one day's work at minimum wage will pay for a blanket. So why invest the time and materials to make a quilt? I would venture that most quilt makers take pride in creating something beautiful. They quilt for the artistic outlet.

Scrap quilts let you express yourself more.

When you make a quilt from 35 identical blocks cut from the same four fabrics, you're done with the creative part after the first block. The next 34 blocks are just pushing a needle. When you make a scrap quilt, you get to savor the creative parts and prolong the artistic decision making. Throughout the process of cutting and piecing, you are making creative choices. Not agonizing choices like which of your children to rescue from a sinking ship or whether to order the molten chocolate or the hot fudge brownie sundae. Just quick, easy, fun choices. Which patch shall I put next to this one? Shall I go for another zinger here? With each seam, you choose fabrics that will work side by side. Each block is a little different, and you will delight in seeing how the quilt develops.

With scrap quilts you are constantly learning.

Not the kind of learning that comes from studying, but the kind that results from happy accidents. The "I-never-would-have-thought-of-putting-those-two-fabrics-together-but-my!-don't-they-look-stunning" kind of learning. If your first block is a dud, you won't need to repeat it over and over. One less-than-perfect block will never be noticed in a scrap quilt. And you can see what doesn't work and do a better job on the next block. Scrap quilts are the best way I know to grow in your art and your use of color. If you allow yourself to employ randomness, even controlled randomness (where you have veto power) in your scrap placement, you will stretch yourself. You may find a whole new direction for your fabric combinations.

Scrap quilts are liberating.

When you use scraps you will never need to worry about yardage again. You won't have to choose between settling for making a quilt smaller than you would like or figuring how to adjust the yardage. If you run out, you can simply buy a few more fat quarters to finish the project.

Scraps make quilts personal.

No two scrap quilts are alike. Even if you made your quilt from a kit, your scrap placement would inevitably differ from everyone else's. All of the little decisions you made will reflect your style.

With scrap quilts you will have something truly special to show for your efforts.

Let's dig into our stashes or hit the quilt shops and see what wonderful scrap quilts we can create!

How to Work with Scraps

When I wrote *Scrap Quilts* in 1985, the fabric selection was not what it is now. Then, fabrics were largely consistent in style. In cotton print fabric, we had small, tone-on-tone prints, and we had more of same. At that time it did not occur to me to discuss scrap selection based on anything but the color and fiber content. I based my own scrap quilts on color families. I suggested pairing clear colors with clear and murky colors with other murky colors. I suggested planning colors according to a theme such as fall or spring, juvenile or sophisticated. While this criteria worked 20 years ago, a new model is needed for today's fabrics.

In the intervening years, fabric availability has changed a great deal. Reproduction fabrics are being manufactured representing 1950s, '30s, Civil War, and pre-Civil War periods. Quilters can also choose from batiks, hand-dyed fabrics, whimsical, Japanese, novelty prints, country style prints and color-wash florals.

My thoughts about combining fabrics for scrap quilts have also changed substantially since 1985. Now I recommend choosing prints by their style, selecting fabrics characteristic of a particular era or ethnicity. For example, you could choose elegant Japanese floral prints or earthy aboriginal Australian or African-inspired patterns. You might think it would be difficult to select fabric for a quilt with so many styles from which to choose. On the contrary, it is easier than ever. Even better, these styles often come with colors in tow. (We have all seen 1930's quilts with their gaily colored pastels.) If you have made a habit of buying fabric that you love, chances are you already have a good start on a scrap quilt in your favored style right in your stash!

Don't limit your palette to a particular line of fabrics. That could give your quilt an over-matched quality. Instead, start with a style. Gather some fabrics in that style and take stock of the range of colors. You can further define your palette by limiting your selections to a color scheme, if you so desire. For example, you can make a quilt in Civil War prints in blues and beiges.

Some fabrics can be incorporated into quilts of several styles. Take your color cues from the prints in your chosen style; then add other fabrics in the same color range.

I think of scrap quilts as a dance of color and pattern, making themes and variations. Through my friendship with Sara Miller, I have been exposed to a beautiful collection of authentic Amish quilts. These quilts are made entirely of solid fabrics, yet the scrap nuances are stunning. The look is achieved by dancing around the colors. The same quilt might include ivory, ecru, dun gray, pale pink, buff, sand, putty, and wheat, along with a similar variety of blues, browns, and purples. These quilts are not made from only bright solids on a black background. Authentic Amish quilts combine murky solids with bright ones. Several variations of a color are used to create nuances in the quilt. Backgrounds can be black or other deep dark colors or they can be grayed medium tones. It is not just bright colors creating the excitement. It is the dance of varying colors, the blending and the contrast, as well as the occasional clash of hues and dash of the unexpected.

The Amish quilt provides an excellent model for a scrap quilt of any style. Dancing around a color is one of my favorite themes for my own quiltmaking—and I rarely use solids. And though at first it took all the courage I could muster, I always incorporate a little bit of a clashing color to enliven the mix.

A few style possibilities for your next scrap quilt are shown on the following page.

Fanfare for the Heroes. *Bright batiks have the nearly solid look needed to define the edges of the stars, but also have the variegation that makes the stars really glow. Small touches of dotty prints add sparkle.*

Newport Beach. *The squares of contemporary fabric have just a hint of print—more of a visual texture, actually. This is ideal for intensifying the colors and contributing to the orderly look of the quilt. The choice of prints also contributes to the shadow illusion by suggesting that the squares have mass, something that would be lost had I used airy prints, for example.*

Celebration. *Bright, whimsical prints with a juvenile attitude color this quilt. These sometimes-busy prints are perfect for a simple pattern like Celebration, where the edges of the patches can run together with impunity. The crisp black and white add definition.*

Hollywood Boulevard. *The style and color cues come from the Japanese-style prints in the large squares. As most of my Japanese scraps were too busy to allow the stars to stand out from the background, I used calicoes and other small prints in similar colors to fashion the star points. (Some of these calicoes had lain dormant in my stash for years just waiting for the perfect quilt!)*

The Red, White, and Blue. *(pattern not available.) This example is made from reproductions of '30s prints, but not in the more widely available pastels. The busy, spotted character of these prints is perfectly balanced with an unbleached solid background. The look is more friendly than sophisticated. The miniature images of puppies, fire trucks, and rolling pins, among others, make a fun I Spy activity for children.*

Three of a Kind. *Floating boxes are fashioned from gilded, swirly, contemporary prints. I began with a few beautiful fabrics by Lonni Rossi. I danced all around them with anything having a similar coloration and spirit. I surprised myself by using an unusual Japanese print (in precisely the right colors) for the background of the quilt.*

The Spanish Steps. *The Nine-Patch squares are made from mid-19th Century reproduction prints with a warm patina. The shadows work in spite of the obvious printed quality of the chains because of the dark values of the prints.*

Cooperstown Stars. *A very scrappy statement is toned down by the low contrast of the country-style prints. The prints have the casual air and warm, golden cast typical of country style.*

7

To gain an understanding of what you like, it can help to look at pictures of quilts. If simply looking doesn't help you define your tastes, try writing down the color combinations of quilts that you like. Use very specific and consistent terms. "Green" isn't as helpful as "olive," or "sea foam green," for example. (I often use the names of the colors in a big box of crayons.) Then look at your color lists and see what they have in common. Using your list as a starting point and adding or subtracting fabrics from there is a great way to plan colors for a scrap quilt.

Artistic rules are made to be broken. I, personally, have broken most of them. That said, many quilters want a starting place, so I will offer several schemes for narrowing color and fabric choices for your quilt based on looks that you may like.

"All" Color Plans

I have seen scrap quilts that seemed to have been made without benefit of any color plans. "Anything goes" seems to be the rule in these quilts. Quilts made in this way tend to have an unschooled, folk-art quality. You may or may not like the look.

I suspect that even quilts made purportedly from all colors have some overriding principles for the selection of fabric. If nothing else, the maker's stash will limit the fabric choices. Most quilt makers' stashes are constrained to the fabrics they like (or liked when they bought them). This fact alone may provide a measure of consistency. If a quilt maker loves (or despises) purple, for instance, the quilt will have an abundance (or a lack) of purple.

I have seen "all"-color scrap quilts that I found quite appealing, but I believe this is the most difficult kind of scrap quilt to make and be pleased with. With no rules at all, it can be hard to make color combinations that sing. I do not personally work in this style, though I have some experience with it, as you can see from the following story.

A friend of mine sought my assistance when she wanted to make her first scrap quilt. She had accumulated scraps from many years of dressmaking. Her "stash" included fabrics representative of many decades, from the '30s to the '90s. She had limited her selection to woven cottons of a weight and weave similar to today's quilting fabrics. This was a good start. She had chosen a quilt pattern and started cutting and sewing before coming to me.

Upon seeing her initial blocks, I was dumbfounded. I had never in my life encountered such a dissonant combination of fabrics! Her patches included everything from florals and novelty prints

from the '30s and '40s to '50s modern motifs, psychedelic '60s, '70s reproductions of old calicoes, tonal prints from the '80s, and contemporary '90 prints of every ilk. Every color imaginable was there: pastels, bright primary colors, dusky tones of mauve gray, and brown, jewel hues, darks from rich to dull, and the world's largest collection of sour chartreuse, apricot, and day-glow pink.

I didn't want to jeopardize our friendship, disrespect my friend's taste, or stunt my friend's growth as a quilter by saying what I thought, so I skirted around the issue by asking what she thought. When it became clear that she was not really happy with the mix, I suggested that we array the fabrics and start removing some of them to judge the effect. I found myself really enjoying this exercise in spite of my initial reaction. We ignored the stylistic attributes as long as the prints provided the necessary contrasts for her chosen pattern. We didn't have any rules. We simply began eliminating colors. Her collected fabrics didn't really need much tweaking. Simply removing a pinkish gray solid that she had been using as a background for all of the blocks made a marked improvement. When we saw the effect of removing the gray, we eliminated the mauve and a few of the duller tones. The bright reds started to stick out like sore thumbs, so we removed those as well. Suddenly, the whole scheme started to work.

A color combination that had looked hopelessly dreadful was transformed into something unique and lovely. I had been making quilts for twenty years, yet I learned as much as my novice friend from this exercise. I liked my friend's quilt so much that I made a quilt in a similar color combination for myself a few years later.

As you can see, we took an all-color palette and pared it down to improve the look. Maybe this kind of quilt plan should simply be called multicolored. Most of us know what we like, even if we don't know it until we see it. And we don't want to give up control of the colors and fabrics in our quilts. So, try as we might, we can't really bring ourselves to include everything in our quilts.

Paint-by-Number Plans

Any design can be made into a scrap quilt. Scraps can do the job of a handful of fabrics, or they can do more. Your scrap plan can echo a non-scrap quilt format. Substitute a variety of blues for a single blue print; numerous yellows for just one; and an assortment of cream, ivory, and off-white prints for the uniform background. I call this approach a paint-by-number plan. Not because it is somehow less than art. Simply because the colors have assigned places in the block and quilt. You can incorporate a consistent accent or background fabric with scraps for the main design elements for a paint-by-number plan, as well.

Block-by-Block Plans

Another way to organize your fabrics for a scrap quilt is a block-by-block plan. Here, you plan colors and fabrics for a single block at a time. You can start with a color scheme or palette, or you can just wing it. A block alone would not look scrappy. However, as each block has a different set of fabrics, the quilt as a whole is scrappy. This is a good plan to use when your quiltmaking time is piecemeal. You can plan and make one or two blocks and put the project aside until later. I will sometimes combine a block-by-block plan with a scrappy background. Both paint-by-number and block-by-block plans serve to limit the scrappy quality of your quilt. I don't generally use a paint-by-number coloring in a block-by-block plan because I prefer a more scrappy look.

Two-Color Plans

You can include the widest range of colors in each position in the quilt if your quilt has a two-color plan. By a two-color plan, I mean that you would sort your fabrics into two groups for placement in the quilt. The quilt may or may not be made from two colors only. Father's Fancy is an example from two colors. Rogue River Log Cabin is a multi-colored example sorted into light and dark values.

Log Cabins, Double Wedding Rings, Drunkard's Paths, and a handful of other designs have two-color plans where the secondary pattern formed when the blocks are joined dominates. In this kind of pattern, the patch does not need defined edges. Patches can just blur together, as long as the overall swath of light and dark is maintained. In this kind of quilt, you can get away with using busy prints, multi-colors, and areas of low contrast and still have an attractive quilt.

Hybrid Plans

Sometimes you can include multiple colors in one position of a paint-by-number plan. Flower Child is basically a paint-by-number plan. However, for the flowers I chose a variety of warm brights from yellow to orange and pink. The star

points in Ring of Fire are made from dark prints of a variety of colors. The rest of the quilt is made in a paint-by-number plan.

You should choose a color plan based on the nature of your quilt pattern. If your block has simple contrasts, a two-color plan adds needed complexity to the look. If, on the other hand, your block has areas of blending as well as areas of strong contrast, you are probably better off with a paint-by-number plan or a block-by-block plan.

How Scrappy is Scrappy Enough for You?

Scrap quilts need not be made entirely from scraps. I find scraps interesting, so my feeling is "the more scraps the merrier." You may have other ideas. Here are a few ways of incorporating scraps.

Scrappy Blocks with One Background Fabric

You may introduce a single fabric as a consistent accent or background for your scrap quilt. This can be done in any kind of scrap quilt, but it is probably seen most often in a two-color plan such as Monet's Wedding Ring. As I mentioned before, Depression-era quilts were typically made from scraps set off by an unbleached solid background. This is a good choice for prints that are too busy for a scrappy background. Japanese prints, whimsical prints, novelty prints, and large florals are similarly busy, and may benefit from a single solid or solid-looking print background as well. Solids tend to stand out in a scrap quilt, so I use them where a consistent accent or a single background fabric is called for. A single background fabric can also be a good choice if your stash is small or you just like to keep the look simple.

Scrappy All Over

A simple all-over pattern entirely of scraps is what I imagine when I hear the word "quilt." The quilt of scrappy stars or other blocks on a similarly scrappy background is another classic look. Both of these looks require a healthy stash. These are the quilts with the best opportunities for adding layers of visual complexity with subtle shadings, dancing around a color, and creative juxtapositions.

Scrappy with a Side of ....

A scrap quilt sometimes benefits from a consistent accent fabric. A Log Cabin quilt with scrappy light and dark logs might have a single red fabric used for the center squares. This adds a punch of color that unifies the quilt.

Examples of different scrap plans and different background treatments are shown at left. From top to bottom:

Father's Fancy. *Two-color quilts are often made with a single background fabric. In this case, the red scraps are not particularly busy prints. However, the high contrast between the reds and the ivory provides plenty of excitement without the addition of scraps in the background.*

Monet's Wedding Ring. *This quilt, too, relies on a plain background for relief. The many colors and busy prints call for a simple treatment. Any two-color design can be interpreted with multi-colored scraps substituted for one of the two colors.*

Ring of Fire. *A single fabric for each of two background areas distinguishes this quilt. It also has scraps sorted into two categories: assorted darks for star points and the ring around them and golds for the ring of squares within each star. It is based on a paint-by-number plan.*

Rogue River Log Cabin. *The scraps for this quilt are sorted into lights and darks. In spite of its many colors, I like to call this kind of quilt a "two-color" quilt because of the two categories for sorting scraps. There is no background here, and both lights and darks are scrappy. The secondary pattern is key here. Two swaths of color form the pattern. It is not necessary to make individual patches stand apart in a Log Cabin design.*

Romeo and Juliet. *This star quilt is made entirely from scraps. The background is especially scrappy. Each star is made from a different set of fabrics, but within a single star the effect is not scrappy at all. I call this kind of scrap placement a block-by-block plan. Each star is principally blue, to offer some continuity.*

Meteor Shower. *This quilt was made in an exceptionally scrappy paint-by-number plan, with each color assigned to a certain area. The background is similar throughout the quilt, but the stars shift in color from one area to another, lending the quilt a contemporary air.*

Grandma's Scrapbook. *This is a more usual interpretation of the paint-by-number plan. Yellow scraps go in the background, purple in the sashes, and so on. A single green fabric is a consistent accent in the center of each block.*

Look through the quilts in this book to see what you like. Determine whether your favorites are more scrappy or less scrappy. Do they have block-by-block, paint-by-number or two-color schemes?

Selecting Fabric for Your Scrap Quilt

Start your fabric selection with pattern in hand and a style in mind. Your chosen style or some favorite fabrics in that style will suggest a color scheme or range of colors. With these colors in mind, begin to select a palette of fabrics for your quilt. Pick fabrics in each color or color range needed for the quilt. Include fabrics with a variety of scales, visual textures, and rhythms. Stretch a little with your colors. You may include fabrics that are not in your chosen style but look good with the other fabrics you have chosen. Every fabric need not be a current favorite. The overall mix is more important than any single fabric.

As you gather fabrics, spread them out in a staggered array to see how they look together. I leave them folded and overlap the fabrics with only an inch or so showing at the fold. Stand back or squint at your array of fabrics. Eliminate any that don't seem to work. If you are not happy with the mix but are not sure what the problem is, start by rearranging the fabrics and removing one color at a time. If removing a color doesn't help the mix, put that color back in and try removing another color. If that helps but you still aren't completely satisfied, try removing a second color.

How many fabrics does it take to make a scrap quilt? The number of different fabrics in a scrap quilt can vary tremendously. Three of a Kind (page 25) has perhaps 25–30 different fabrics. The small quilt size, single background fabric, and block-by-block coloring all limit the number of fabrics needed. On the other end of the scale, Fanfare for the Heroes (page 107) and Meteor Shower (page 45) might have hundreds of fabrics. Their scrappy backgrounds and nuanced shading of diamonds within a star point call for a large and varied palette. How scrappy a quilt looks depends more on the number of different colors, the uniformity of color placement, and how far each color ranges than on the number of different fabrics included.

The two-color quilt, Father's Fancy (page 95), has a single background fabric and a large number of different red prints. However, the range of colors is limited, and the type of print is consistent. The quilt does not look exceptionally scrappy. Monet's Wedding Ring (page 37) also has a single background fabric. The quilt looks scrappier despite a similar number of fabrics because the prints include a variety of colors and values and the prints are busier.

When I am making a scrap quilt, I don't start out with a certain number of fabrics in mind. The number depends on what I have on hand and what I can find at my favorite quilt shops to supplement my stash. Often, I will adjust my fabric selection according to the cutting requirements of the pattern. For example, if I am making a twin-sized Hollywood Boulevard (page 64), and I have gathered 35 different Japanese prints, I might leave out one of them. This leaves 34 fabrics, the number of strips required to cut the A squares. I can simply cut one strip from each of the fabrics.

If I am making a wall-sized Rogue River Log Cabin (page 53), I might scrounge up three dark fabrics to bring the 45 that I had initially up to 48, half the number of strips required. If I had only 21 lights, I might cut four strips from each fabric and cut an extra strip from two of the fabrics to total the 86 strips required.

I usually use 100 or more fabrics in a single scrap quilt. For color-by-number quilts, I will select a minimum of 50 prints for each color in the plan. I will array the fabrics I am considering and kick out any that stick out like a sore thumb. I may cut just enough scraps to make a test block. When I am satisfied with that, I will cut out all of the patches.

For block-by-block quilts, I choose fabric for one to four blocks at a time. Each block has its own color scheme, with a general range for the quilt's main colors determined in advance. Accent colors in a block may stray beyond the range for the main colors. For this type of quilt, I might use each fabric in just one block.

My yardage and fat quarter requirements for the patterns in this book list the minimum amount of fabric that you will use to make the quilt. To match the scrappy effect in my quilts, you will need to use small amounts of many more prints.

Rotary Cutting Fat Quarters

For a scrap quilt, select four fat quarters from which you plan to cut the same patches. Press enough of each fabric to cut the needed strips. Stack them to make four layers. Because there is no fold, the fabrics lay perfectly flat and are easier to align and cut precisely. Align the edges parallel to the selvage (which should have been trimmed off already). Fat quarters may vary slightly in length. Arrange the stacked fabrics with one crosswise edge fairly even and the other less so. Press again, this time through all four layers. Let the fabric cool slightly before transferring it to your cutting mat. (Your mat can warp if you place hot fabric on it.) Trim off ⅛" from the aligned lengthwise edge through all four layers. I call this a clean cut. It assures a precise cut from each layer. Then measure and cut the widest strip parallel to the clean cut. Wide strips can be cut down to the next smaller size when you have cut a sufficient number of the larger patches. I sometimes cut just one strip from each fabric. The shorter (18") length of lengthwise strips allows for more scrap variety than 44" crosswise strips permit.

If you are cutting a Log Cabin or other pattern requiring several patches of the same width but varying lengths, cut an assortment of patch lengths from each strip. If you cut the longest patches first, the shorter ones can often be cut from the leftovers. Furthermore, you don't want all of your green floral patches to be in the same place in the various blocks. Cutting a variety of patches from a strip maximizes the scrappy quality of your quilt.

Cutting Patches from Scraps and Remnants

If the fabric has a selvage, trim off the selvage and cut strips parallel to it. If the piece no longer has a selvage, determine the lengthwise grain by pulling two ends of the fabric along the threads, first in one direction, then the other. The less stretchy grain is the lengthwise grain. Cut following a lengthwise thread, which may be more readily evident on the back side of the fabric. Sometimes it is easier to follow the print, aligning your ruler with the same part of the printed motif at each repeat. If the scrap is large enough to cut multiple rows of patches, I usually start by making a clean cut following the lengthwise grain down the middle of the scrap. This gives me two pieces, each with a clean edge. I stack these and cut through two layers at once.

Scrap Pairings

Some quilters audition each patch on a design wall. Most don't agonize over every little decision, though. Usually, a quick and easy judgment will do. For most of my quilts, I don't expend much effort deciding where to put each patch. I don't audition them on a design wall. I like the "happy accidents" that result from cutting a bunch of patches and just taking the top patch from each of two piles and seeing how they look together. If it isn't pretty, I simply substitute the second patch for one of them....and so on.

When I have a fabric that I feel will be harder to pair with others, I sew these first, while I still have plenty of options left.

Even if you plan to be completely random about it, I think you will find yourself sometimes vetoing patch combinations and looking for something more suitable. After all, this is your quilt, and you want it to be just so. Every decision makes your quilt a little more of a personal statement. Every choice you make affects the whole. Every detail that you consider (and some that you don't even think about) becomes a thread in the intricate weave of the quilt surface.

Building a Fabric Stash

Obviously, it is helpful to have a stash of fabrics on hand if you plan to make scrap quilts. If you try to build a scrap quilt from the fabrics you can find at the store at any given moment, you will probably end up with an imperfect mix. Too many fabrics will be from over-matched, coordinated lines; you'll have the same prints in several colors; and you may not be able to find some colors at all.

I have a large stash of fabric built over the last 36 years. I sometimes shop with a specific project in mind, planning to augment my stash. Often, I simply draw from my stash to make a quilt. I shop for fabrics I love, fabrics to fill in color gaps in my stash, and fabrics to replace ones I have (heaven forbid!) used up. I generally buy half yards and fat quarters. This was not always the case. When I was a new quilter (and cotton fabric was scarce and cheap—$1.29 per yard), I used to buy 3 yards if I loved a fabric (enough for a border on a bed-sized quilt) and 9 yards if I liked it and it was on sale. (Looking at my stash with hindsight, I sometimes think I must have bought 1 yard if I didn't like a fabric.) Now I have so much fabric in my stash that finding room for more can be a problem.

Build your stash over a period of time, buying when you see something you like, or buying to fill gaps in your collection. Before long, you will have a fabric collection with depth and variety that will make your quilts sing.

You don't have to collect every style of fabric. Start with the one or two styles that best suit your personality. I started with calicoes; eased into reproduction fabrics, toiles, and florals; batiks and contemporary and Japanese prints came later.

If you are trying to build a stash from scratch, start with half-yard lengths. A quarter yard will get used up with the first quilt. Bigger cuts cost more and will limit the variety you can afford to pay for or to store.

Buy extra fabric whenever you make a project. You won't have to worry about running short, and the extra will make a great addition to your stash. I like to buy everything I am considering for a project. That way, I can make my final selection from the comfort of my own home. I can even make a sample block before making my final decision. I once bought 35 yards of fabric for a 36" square wall quilt. I never expected to use it all in the one quilt. I knew the fabric would make a good addition to my stash.

Buy fabric just because you love it. (What a delightful idea!) There is no need to feel guilty when it is for your stash. Buy it when it is on sale. Buy it when you are on vacation and have set aside money for souvenirs. Buy when you need inspiration. Sometimes a beautiful new fabric is all it takes to jumpstart your creativity.

Ask for fabric or for gift certificates to your favorite quilt shop for birthdays, anniversaries, and other occasions. If asking outright doesn't fly in your family, try hinting.

Fabric shopping just might be the best part of making quilts. (Some people who call themselves quilt makers never get beyond collecting the fabric!) Buying for your stash is best of all because you don't have to limit your choices to things that go together. You might get some funny looks when your selection appears to have been made blindfolded. (I always feel I need to explain myself when the fabrics I am purchasing don't go together. I worry that someone might think I have awful taste.) If you have a twisted sense of humor, you might see how far you can go with disparate choices before someone tries to steer you in another direction.

Storing Your Stash

For my scraps, I have shoe-box-sized plastic boxes arranged on a bookcase beside my cutting table. Each box is labeled with a finished size. I store all shapes in one box, using dividers to separate the different shapes. I keep the patches neatly stacked, something I have found to be crucial if you ever want to use these scraps in a quilt. Half-square triangles are put into the box for their finished short side; quarter-square triangles are sorted according to the dimensions of their finished long sides. These are easy for me to remember because they correspond to the straight grain. And the 3" quarter-square triangle is easy to distinguish from the 3" half-square triangle, which is much larger. Rectangles are sorted based on their width (short side). I also store leftover strips and strip ends in the box with same-sized patches. I pin labels to strips to indicate their cut width.

If I want to make a test block, I find that I usually have enough patches already cut out in my labeled boxes. I also use these precut patches when I need one or two more patches when I run out or need more choices when I am close to running out. I used to keep messy bins of strip ends and fabrics

too small to fold. I seldom used these fabrics, however. Now, I cut these ends into common patch sizes and shapes and file them away. I find that I am much more likely to dip into these boxes to find precut patches.

Many practical and attractive options are available for your scrap and fat quarter storage. Depending on your personal style, you could use boxes or bins made of plastic, wire, metal, wood, mesh, rattan, or cardboard covered with linen, leather, or wallpaper. You could also use baskets or drawers. Desktop organizers, cutlery trays, or mini-bins are helpful for dividing drawers into suitable cubbyholes for various-sized patches.

My yardage and fat quarters are sorted into batik and contemporary fabrics; '30s reproductions; 19th Century reproductions plus calicoes, small florals, and toiles; Japanese-inspired fabrics; French Provincial; and larger pieces for backings, borders, and bindings. Within a style, the fabric is sorted by color. I sort fabrics having light backgrounds according to their background color, without regard to the color of the printed figures.

Over the years I have stored my stash in different ways depending on my circumstances. I started out sewing in the laundry room with fabric stored on open shelves. For a time, my sewing was in a bedroom, with my stash in a closet fitted with plywood shelving. Then I had a basement sewing room with a walk-in closet designed specifically for fabric storage. My current sewing room is an over-the-garage space with a sloped ceiling. I had a 20-foot-long counter built in with open storage underneath. Initially, I stored fabric under the counter. Gradually I have converted that space to storage for batting and other bulky items. My stash now resides in inexpensive pre-fabricated bookcases lining the hall and adjacent alcove just outside my sewing room. The space is perfect for fabric: windowless with overhead lighting to make it easy to find what I am looking for. This space is roomier than a walk-in closet and feels open, though it is not in the line of sight of visitors or even family members unless they are coming to the sewing room. Large project tubs are close at hand under my ironing table to organize the fabric, cut patches, notes, and sewn bits of the several quilts that I am working on at any time.

So far, I have managed with build-it-yourself bookcases, scratch-and-dent office furniture, and the like. I sometimes dream of doing something more elegant if I had the time and money. But I'd probably rather spend my money on fabric when it comes right down to it.

How to Make a Quilt

In this chapter, I will give an overview of basic rotary cutting, machine piecing, and hand quilting. I'll include some tips especially for scrap quilts and details about some of the techniques used to make the quilts in this book. Find instructions for set-in seams, partial seams, point trimming, and more.

Basic Rotary Cutting Tools

Good patchwork begins with good tools. You'll need three tools to start rotary cutting:

1. a rotary cutter and extra blades
2. a cutting mat
3. a long, wide rotary ruler

The rotary cutter looks like a pizza cutter, with a wheel blade attached to a handle. However, it is razor-sharp. Always exercise caution when using a rotary cutter. Use the blade guard when you are not cutting. If you talk with your hands, for goodness sake, put your cutter down before you open your mouth. Keep your fingers well clear of the edge of the ruler when cutting. And, finally, cut from side to side or away from your body, rather than toward it. Keep your cutting area clear of papers, pins, and other materials because anything on your cutting mat will invariably jump into the path of your blade, probably ruining both the blade and your child's homework or whatever got in the way.

The cutting mat provides a tough work surface that not only protects your table from the blade, but also preserves the blade. Choose a self-healing mat, as the cuts in the mat naturally close, leaving little or no scarring of the surface. Most mats have a grid of one-inch squares printed on them with measurements around the edges. This is not the boon you might think. Using the mat's rule lines doubles your work. Carefully aligning the fabric with the mat as well as the ruler takes twice as long as simply plopping down your fabric without regard to the mat's rulings, and aligning your ruler with the fabric. Mats can warp and ripple when exposed to heat. Don't leave them in a hot car, and don't even think about ironing on them. Store them flat when not in use.

Your ruler should be made specifically for rotary cutting. Fine, crisp lines improve your accuracy, and dashed lines help you see the edge of your fabric under the line. Your basic ruler should be as small as possible and as big as necessary to cut the strips you desire. If you cut lengthwise strips from half yards or fat quarters, as I do, a ruler 18" to 24" in length and 6" to 8" in width is perfect. Rulers

with few lines may lack rulings for some of your most common strip sizes, such as the 2⅞" strip needed to cut 2" finished triangles. I personally like a grid of ⅛" squares on a ruler. Your basic ruler should have a 45° angle printed on it.

The Long and the Short of Lengthwise Strips

I recommend cutting strips 18" long for use in scrap quilts. Not only are they perfect for the fat quarters and half-yard cuts of fabric so often used for scrap quilts, but also, being shorter than your usual crosswise strips, they offer maximum scrap variety. These short strips run parallel to the selvage along the lengthwise grain. You may want to use these lengthwise strips for all your patchwork once you see how well the strips follow the print and how much less stretchy they are.

You don't have to throw out everything you've learned about rotary cutting to start using short lengthwise strips today. Everything is the same except the length of your strips and the direction that you turn the fabric when you cut it.

How to Cut Lengthwise Short Strips

Lengthwise strips have the long side of the strip parallel to the selvedge. Strips can be cut any length, but I generally use 18" strips. Before you layer fabrics and cut strips, trim off the selvages. I do this by placing the ruler's ½" line along the selvage, and cutting on the ruler's edge. If you have prewashed your fabric, the selvage may shrink and

curl. If this is the case, you can make short snips in the selvage to straighten the edge enough to trim off the selvage, (along with the snips) or you can trim a few inches at a time, realigning your ruler as often as it takes to get a straight cut. As you cut strips, you may place the fabric with the long, trimmed edge and lengthwise grain parallel to the front edge of the cutting table, and cut from right to left or from left to right. I use this method because I am directionally challenged, and I can never remember which way the fabric goes with any other method. If you prefer, you may place the fabric with the crosswise grain parallel to the front edge of the table, and cut away from your body.

For a scrap quilt, press at least the part of the fabric that you will be using, and stack four different fabrics to make four layers. Because there is no fold, the fabrics lay perfectly flat and are easy to cut precisely. Align the trimmed side and one end of the fabrics. I like to press the fabric again as a stack, and trim off ⅛" or so. This assures that all strips will be the same size. I sometimes cut just one strip from each fabric.

If you will be cutting many strips from the same long yardage, you may cut the fabric into 18" lengths (or any other length up to the length of your ruler if you prefer). You can stack the pieces for up to four layers and cut as described above.

Rotary Cutting Patches

For scrap quilts, rotary cutting the patches allows you to place each fabric exactly where you want it. You can make your blocks and quilts without once duplicating a patch combination. Rotary cutting shapes is fast and efficient. Layer four fabrics. Cut a single stack of strips first. Leave the strip stack in place on the mat, and pull the remaining fabric an inch or so away from your patches. Trim the aligned crosswise end of the strip to square it up or cut it off at an angle as listed.

You may need to rotate the strip to begin sub cuts. Usually, sub cuts (subsequent cuts) are parallel to the squared or angled end cut. Position the rule line listed for your patch over the trimmed end of the strip. Make a sub cut parallel to the end at the listed interval. If you will be making further sub cuts, gently slide the strip between cuts to allow space between units.

Continue with the subsequent cuts described for your shape. These cuts may involve cutting the unit in half diagonally or cutting off one or more corners, for example. When you sub cut strips into squares or other shapes, keep the handling to a minimum. Leave the strip in place and turn the ruler and/or mat as needed. Complete the patch cutting for one strip before going on to the next.

While the patches are still in neat stacks of four, trim points according to pattern directions. After the patches are completely cut and trimmed, set them aside and proceed with additional strips and patches from the same fabrics. When you have cut all strips and patches from one stack of fabrics, go on to another stack of fabrics.

Try rotary cutting patches. It's easy. It's versatile. And it gives you total freedom in the placement of your scrap fabrics.

Practical Point Trimming

Grandma trimmed her points, but she did it after piecing. Her object was to reduce bulk in seams and minimize show-through. Works for me, but trimming before you sew can do more. Grandma aligned patches by drawing stitching lines. We can align patches by pretrimming points.

I discovered the advantages of point trimming 35 years ago quite by accident. I didn't know a quilt from a quintet. Someone told me that quilts were made with ¼" seam allowances. Through some perversity of understanding, I trimmed my seam allowances down to ¼" at the points. My earliest quilts went together easily. Later, when I found out how quilts were supposed to be made, I decided to skip the point trimming. Big mistake! I was making a Lone Star. It was a bear to put together. Without the trims, I had a hard time getting the diamonds to line up right. I couldn't get back to my own methods soon enough.

Trimming the excess from sharp points before sewing yields neater, easier, and more accurate patchwork. It also helps you keep seam allowances even by eliminating dog ears, those distracting triangles of fabric that stick out past the edge of the seam allowances.

The full-size pattern pieces in this book show how the points should be trimmed. A Point Trimmer tool will help for trimming points of typical triangles, trapezoids, diamonds, and parallelograms having 45° angles. Simply align the converging lines of the triangle on the tool with the point of your patch. (Your patch doesn't have to match the

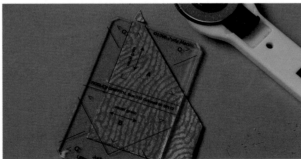

size of the triangle on the tool. Your patch doesn't even have to be a triangle. It just has to have the same angle.) Use your rotary cutter to trim off the bit that extends beyond the ruler at the point.

Reverse Psychology

Most of the common patches, such as squares and rectangles, are symmetrical; they look the same face up or face down. These can be cut right or left handed, with fabric folded in half or not, with the same results. Some other patches, such as long triangles, parallelograms, and half trapezoids, are asymmetrical. Take special care to cut these asymmetrical patches according to plan.

Some quilts call for asymmetrical patches and their reverses in equal quantities. These are mirror images; cut both at the same time from fabric folded in half. These can also be cut from stacked fabrics, half of them face up and half face down. Sometimes all asymmetrical patches in a quilt are alike. In such a case, you must not fold the fabric. Furthermore, care must be taken to keep stacked fabrics all facing the same side up.

Simply Sixteenths

In the past, sixteenths didn't come up much. Sometimes, numbers were merely rounded to the nearest eighth (Horrors!). And sometimes designs were avoided if they had sixteenths. You can make some really neat patterns if you are willing to measure sixteenths, and it isn't really any harder than any other measurement. Since quilters are more accustomed to eighths than sixteenths, and most rotary rulers do not indicate sixteenths, I have a different way of designating these measurements.

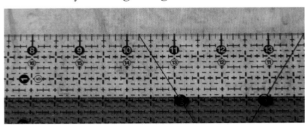

Sixteenths fall halfway between two neighboring eighths. In this book, $\frac{1}{16}$ inches are designated the way you would use your ruler to cut them. That is, the book lists the next lower eighth followed by a "+." For example, $1\frac{1}{16}$", which is halfway between 1" and $1\frac{1}{8}$", would be listed as 1+".

Aim for Accuracy

My approach to patchwork is to aim for accuracy. It is based on my inherent laziness and my total inability to deal with frustration. I don't want to do anything over again. I don't imagine you want to do anything over again, either.

I have seen people slap that rotary ruler down so fast that I wonder how they managed to land it on the fabric! What's the big hurry? Can't they wait

16

to get to the sewing headaches that will inevitably ensue? You can make up the little extra time it takes to measure carefully when you avoid fussing and finagling later.

Hold your ruler firmly in place, walking your hand down the ruler as you cut. Your cutter will be pushing against the ruler, so you need to steady the ruler alongside the blade (but not too close!) Cut through no more than four layers. Keep the blade straight up and down, not tilted, in order to ensure that top and bottom layers are the same size.

Most students' accuracy problems are not a matter of cutting, however. It is the seam allowances that most often cause the problems. Most people err on the side of seam allowances that are too deep. If you need to fine tune your seam allowances, get a good idea of how much to adjust them by doing this exercise: Cut out nine $1\frac{1}{2}$" squares and one $1\frac{1}{2}$" x $9\frac{1}{2}$" rectangle from one of your uglier fabrics. Stitch the squares end to end. Press, being careful to avoid tucks. Pin and sew the long side of the rectangle to the long side of the strip of squares. (No fair easing!) If the two halves are even on both ends, congratulations! Your seam allowances are great. If the rectangle extends beyond the squares, your seam allowances are too deep. If the squares stick out beyond the rectangle, your seam allowances are too shallow.

If your seam allowance is a mere $\frac{1}{32}$" too deep, each square will be $\frac{1}{16}$" too small. With 8 such seams, your strip of squares will be $\frac{1}{2}$" too small. A full-sized quilt could be as much as 6" too small using this scenario! Of course, your seam allowance is probably not that far off. The problem with any one seam is likely to be barely measurable. A matter of a couple of threads' width can make all the difference.

Seam allowances that are too deep result in a smaller quilt, but that is only the tip of the iceberg. The bigger problem is the way different parts no longer fit together. Borders don't fit the quilt center, sashes don't fit the blocks, and the large patches don't fit the units made up of smaller patches. It's irritating when nothing fits. Learning to get it right from the start is a one-time effort that pays off with every quilt you make.

The Perfect Seam Gauge

Many quilters use the edge of their presser foot as a seam gauge. There are special patchwork feet for this purpose. Other quilters follow a $\frac{1}{4}$" mark etched on the throat plate of their machines. My machine has a so-called $\frac{1}{4}$" line, but it does not make an accurate seam allowance for piecing. In patchwork, a little fabric is taken up at each seam. You lose a bit due to the thickness of the thread and the bulk of the material. In order to adjust for this take up, you will want your seam allowances to be just a thread or two shy of ¼" (a scant ¼"). My preferred seam guide is a piece of tape on the throat plate. This provides a slightly raised edge that helps you guide the fabric accurately.

To make your own tape seam guide, carefully trace or photocopy one of the templates from the book. Include both seam lines and cutting lines. Cut out your copy on the inside edge of the cutting lines, in effect, cutting off the solid lines. (Cutting off the line of the template adjusts your seam allowance for take up.) If you photocopy, verify that the copy is accurately sized by laying the copy over the corresponding template in the book.

Insert the needle of your sewing machine into the seam line marked on the paper copy. Lower the presser foot, and stitch (with or without thread) for an inch or so to make sure that the needle is following the seam line exactly. (Raise the presser foot, and straighten the pattern if necessary.)

When you are satisfied that the needle is going straight down the seam line, leave the presser foot down, and place a piece of black electrical tape on the throat plate of the machine directly alongside the cut edge of the pattern piece. (The electrical tape lasts longer than masking tape before going all gummy on you.) Remove the pattern piece.

When you sew, keep the patches of fabric even with the edge of the tape. If your sewing machine's feed dogs are where the tape needs to be, you can use the edge of the presser foot as your guide or move the needle position to the right to allow you to place the tape to the right of the feed dogs.

Preparation for Sewing

For machine sewing, set your stitch length at about ten stitches per inch. Use a size 11 needle for cottons of the weight typically used for quilts. My favorite thread is Aurofil 50-weight, a silky-smooth 100% cotton thread that is fine enough for me to thread in spite of my aging eyes. Choose a neutral thread color. I use beige for quilts with a golden cast and silvery gray for quilts that have a blue cast. I don't change thread color as I piece the quilt top. I do change thread color to match the fabric when joining binding strips, long border strips, or backing panels. Wind several bobbins in advance so you won't lose your momentum when your bobbin runs out, and you won't need to rethread your machine so often.

Pin Pointers

If you are having trouble with the joints of your patchwork, it just might be on account of your pins. Pins that are too thick, too long, or have a large head may make too much of a hump in the seam line. The best pins for patchwork are very fine (0.5 mm) and pretty short (1¼" or so).

Pinning is essential to sewing success whenever seams are long or have joints to match. I always pin borders, bindings, lining panels, and block rows at every joint and no more than four inches apart. I pin even short seams if they have joints. I usually stitch over the pins, though I know that crunching pins is hard on your sewing machine. I should probably tell you to remove the pin when the needle reaches the joint. There. I've said it.

Sewing

Place patches with right sides together and cut edges aligned. Pin as needed. Align the cut edges of patches with the seam guide, and stitch from edge to edge of the patches. Back stitch at the ends of seams. Back tacking becomes a habit, and it takes very little time and effort. It is essential to back tack patchwork that will be at the edge of the quilt top, as seams may unravel with handling or when the quilt is mounted for quilting.

Chain Piecing

Chain piecing allows you to stitch one seam after another without cutting the thread. You can stitch as fast or as slowly as you like. You can back tack at both ends of each seam. You simply join two patches in a seam, stitching from edge to edge. You come to a stop and leave the presser foot down. Insert another pair of patches under the tip of the presser foot. Don't cut the thread. You can stitch through thin air for a couple of stitches if you need to. Chain piecing conserves thread and makes it unnecessary to snip off threads later. Units will be connected by a twist of thread. When you complete a step, use thread snips to cut units apart. Some people insert a scrap to stitch and leave under the needle when they want to snip apart the units, including the last one. I prefer to insert an actual pair of patches. If you are going to be stitching, why not stitch on a quilt? Keep patches for a simple project handy, and you can make progress on two quilts at once.

Assembly-line Strategies

With assembly-line piecing, you chain piece all of one unit before proceeding to the next unit. This can be very efficient, as you only have to think once about what goes next, which way to turn patches, which side to stitch, and so on. If you use this method, be careful. You can repeat a mistake many times before you realize it!

I get impatient with assembly-line work because I am always eager to see results. I usually repeat a step just enough to make a block or two. I'll then go on to the next step. I'll complete one or two blocks and go back to the beginning for the next block or two.

Assembly-line work is more interesting for scrap quilts. You get to break up the monotony by choosing different fabrics. I make piles of the two kinds of patches to be joined in a step. I'll take the top patch from one pile and try it with the top patch of the other pile. If I like the pairing, I'll stitch it and go on to the next pair. If I don't like the two together, I'll substitute the next patch for one of the two. Sometimes, it becomes apparent that one print is hard to pair with the others. In these cases, I try to stitch these first, while there are still plenty of possible pairings to choose from.

Joints and Points

Generally, patchwork seam allowances are pressed to one side rather than being pressed open. This keeps the batting from seeping through the spaces between the stitches. It also forms ridges that will help you align seams perfectly at joints. In preparation for stitching across a joint, finger press seam allowances in opposite directions. Hold the joint between your thumb and forefinger and slide the two halves until they stop at the ridge formed by the seam allowances. At this point, the joint

matches perfectly. Stick a pin in at an angle across both sets of seam allowances, and stitch. If I cannot oppose the seam allowances at a joint, I will

18

oppose seams just to find the perfect alignment. Then I'll flip the twisted seam allowance back and insert a pin to hold it in place.

One mistake beginners commonly make is to think that points should be at the edge of the block even before the block is sewn to another one. Actually, the points should be ¼" in from the raw edges of the block so they won't get chopped off when you sew the block to the next one. Your

points will naturally be ¼" from the edge if your seam allowances are accurate. Each point should have two lines of stitching crossing on the back of the work. When you sew the block to the next unit, your stitching should go right across the point where the two seam lines cross.

Pressing and Finger Pressing

Be careful not to stretch bias edges out of shape when you press. Use a dry iron and press only in the direction of the straight grain of the fabric. Until the blocks are done, I finger press only. To do this, lay the unit, right side up, on your thigh. Run your thumbnail along the seam line to train the seam allowance to one side. Wooden pressing sticks are available to substitute for your thumbnail, but I prefer to feel the seam and make sure I get the seam line fully open.

Use common sense when deciding which way to press seam allowances. Press away from the bulk. That is, if you are sewing a single patch to a seamed unit, press the seam allowances toward the single patch. At a point, never press both seam allowances toward the point. Where many points come together, press all seam allowances clockwise (or all counter-clockwise) so that they will oppose each other. Even if it means pressing toward the bulk, press at least one seam of every patch away from the patch to keep it from billowing.

Set-In Seams

Set-in seams or Y-seams are nothing to fear. If you cut and stitch accurately, your set-in patches will fall into place naturally. The important thing to remember about set-in patches is that you must not stitch over the seam allowances at the joint. The seam allowances need to be free to pivot in order for the joint to lie flat. You will have to stitch a Y-seam in two passes: from the joint to one side and from the joint to the other side. I usually put a pin where I need to start the first line of stitching. For the second pass, the first line of stitching marks my starting point.

Most set-in seams involve two like patches and one different one. I usually sew first one, then the other of the matching patches to the different one. The final seam, then, is the one joining the two matching patches. Because they match, it is easier to align these patches perfectly for the final seam.

Partial Seams

Partial seams are used when a joint is crossed by a straight seam, but you need to make the seam in two passes because one of the two segments you are joining extends beyond the other. These seams are easy to do. You simply start sewing at the end of the seam where the segments are the same length, but you stop sewing before you get to the

uneven end. When you get further along, and the two segments are now even, you may complete the partial seam, stitching from where you stopped before to the edge. The only hard thing about partial seams is knowing when to use them. I make it easy for you in this book. When you see a solid pink line turning into a dashed pink line at a pink dot, a partial seam is called for. Start stitching at the solid end of the line. Stop stitching at the pink dot. Complete the dashed seam line later. That's all there is to it!

Setting the Quilt Together

After you have made all of the blocks, you simply join the blocks in rows, then join the rows.

Be sure to pin the seams liberally. If the quilt is set with sashing, insert short sashing strips between blocks in a row. Between rows of blocks, insert long sashes (or piece together short sashes and setting squares and insert them).

Attaching Borders

The border sizes listed in my patterns are exact lengths with seam allowances included. If your patchwork is accurate, the borders should not need to be trimmed to fit. Once you have mastered an accurate seam allowance, the best way to achieve border fit is to make borders the size listed, and pin the centers and ends of the border to the quilt top. Then proceed to pin every few inches. You should not need to do any easing. For abutted borders, pin, then sew a strip to one edge of the quilt, then the opposite edge. Pin and sew the other two strips to the remaining edges Attach additional borders in a similar fashion.

If you are not so confident in your seam allowances and want to measure the quilt, measure it across the center as well as along the sides. Adjust the length of your border strips by the difference between your measurements and the listed border lengths. Pin before stitching borders to the quilt.

For mitered corners, once again, the easiest way to fit the borders is to sew accurately and use the sizes listed. If you need to adjust borders to fit your quilt, add or subtract the difference between your measurement and the listed size. Then cut off both ends of each border from the corner at a 45° angle before pinning and stitching the border to the quilt. Stitch to ¼" from the edge. (You sew mitered corners as you would a Y-seam.) After attaching borders to all four sides of the quilt, pin and stitch the miters together at the corners.

For multiple mitered borders, first pin and join multiple border strips in sequence, matching centers and ends. Then cut off the corners of the whole set of borders at a 45° angle. Then proceed as described above.

Choosing a Quilting Pattern

The object of quilting is to hold the layers together and to add another decorative element. The most common kinds of quilting are in the ditch, outline, fill, and decorative motifs. In-the-ditch quilting is directly beside the seam lines on the side without the seam allowances. It is done by eye, without marking. This quilting defines the edges of the pieced patches.

Outline quilting also defines the edges of patches, but the stitches are more easily seen.

Quilting stitches run ¼" in from the seam lines of the patch. You can outline quilt by eye or you can follow the edge of a strip of masking tape.

Curved quilting complements the straight lines of patchwork nicely. Wide plain borders and sashes, alternate plain blocks, and other large patches are good places to show off fancy quilting. Choose a design for the largest areas first. Often, the same motif can be adapted to fit other parts of the quilt. You can mark these designs with a stencil after basting, or you can trace the designs with the aid of a light box before basting layers. Some quilters can do freehand motifs without marking.

Filler quilting is used to hold down the background to allow the decorative quilting motifs to stand out. It can be done with grids, parallel lines, or radiating lines marked with masking tape after basting. Filler quilting also includes stippling or small meandering stitches that are done by eye.

If you will be sending your top out for quilting by a professional, ask the quilter her ideas for quilting. She knows what she likes to do and does well. I generally recommend stitching in the ditch around stars and other shapes and stitching down the background with a filler. You will want a different quilting plan for machine quilting than you would choose for hand quilting. With hand quilting, straight lines that can be marked with masking tape are easy; going over seam allowances is hard. With machine quilting, straight lines and lots of starts and stops are hard.

Marking for Quilting

If you will be sending your top out for quilting, the quilter will most likely do the marking, if any. If you will be using a quilting stencil, you can mark and quilt a few motifs at a time after the layers are basted. If you will be using a drawing instead of a stencil, start by tracing the design onto white paper with a black felt pen. Tape the tracing, face up, onto a light box or a glass table top, and place the quilt top, also face up, over it. Adjust the quilt top to position the motif as desired. Turn on the light box or place a lamp under the glass table top to help you see the pattern clearly through the fabric. Mark each patch and border motif according to your plan.

Layering and Basting

Now you are ready to make the quilt backing and layer the top, batting, and backing. Make the backing about 8" longer and 8" wider than your quilt top in order to allow for mounting it for quilting. The sizes listed in my patterns allow for

20

the extra 8". Unless your quilt is very small or you are using extra-wide backing material, you will have to join two or three lengths of material to make your backing. Trim the selvages off the yard goods before cutting out the panels. Cut out the quilt panels as listed in the pattern. Make a fresh cut at the end of the length of backing fabric to square it up. Use a square ruler or a long, wide one to make sure the corners are square. Cut each panel precisely the same length and width. Pin and stitch panels together with ¼" seam allowances. Press seam allowances to one side. Press the quilt top and backing well. Snip any stray threads.

Place the backing face down on a large, flat surface such as the floor or a ping-pong table. Spread the batting evenly over it. Smooth the quilt top, centered face up, over the backing and batting. Pin through all three layers. Some quilters use safety pins for this purpose. I prefer to use long straight pins and remove them after basting. Baste in a large X across the quilt; then baste lines about six inches apart across and down the quilt. Also baste around the edges. Try to avoid basting precisely where the quilting stitches will be.

Quilting

I recommend taking a class to learn hand or machine quilting. If you have never watched an experienced quilter at work, try to arrange to do so. Sign up for a class or join a guild.

For hand quilting, mount your quilt in a frame or large hoop. Cut off an 18"–24" length of thread. Thread a needle with a single strand and no knot. Take a stitch along one of your intended quilting lines. Pull the thread to its halfway point, leaving a tail free to continue stitching later. Rather than grasping the needle between thumb and index finger, push the needle from the eye end with a thimble on your middle finger. Use your thumb to

depress the fabric in front of the needle, and use your other hand under the quilt to help guide the fabric onto the needle. Stack several stitches on the needle before pulling the needle through. Try for even stitches. Short stitches will come with time. When you reach the end of the thread, take a small back stitch. Then run the needle through the batting alongside the line of quilting, where it won't work loose with handling. Bring the needle back out an inch or so away. Snip the thread directly at the surface of the quilt top and let the thread end slip back between the layers. Thread the remaining half of the thread, and continue quilting.

Binding

In preparation for binding, use a rotary cutter and ruler to trim the batting and backing even with the quilt top. Take special care to achieve right angles at the corners. Cut the binding fabric into straight strips (or bias) 2" wide and in sufficient quantity to go around the quilt's perimeter with several inches to spare. (These patterns allow at least 8" extra.) Trim the ends of the strips at a 45° angle, with all ends parallel to one another when the strips are all right side up. Trim the points to help you align the strips for seaming. Pin and stitch the strips end to end with ¼" seam allowances to make one long strip. Press these seam allowances open. Fold the strip in half lengthwise with right sides out. Press the fold for the full length of the strip.

Starting on one edge of the quilt (and not near the corner), lay the folded binding strip over one edge of the quilt, with the pieced side of the quilt face up. Start about 4"–6" from one end of the binding. Align the raw edges of the two layers of binding with the cut edges of the quilt top, and pin through both layers of binding plus the quilt top, batting, and backing. Pin and stitch just one side of the quilt, stopping ¼" from the raw edge of the next side of the quilt. Wrap the binding around to the back of the quilt at the corner, even with binding on the front. Crease the binding crosswise

at the quilt's raw edge. Now bring this creased edge to the front of the quilt and align the crease with the raw edge of the part you just stitched. Pin at the corner, then pin along the entire next side.

Stitch from ¼" from the crease in the binding at one corner to ¼" from the raw edge at the next corner. Back tack at the ends of the seam.

Repeat this process until you have stitched the binding to all sides and around all corners. Stop stitching 4"–6" short of your starting point. Lay the starting end of the binding strip over the quilt top, and pin it to the edge of the quilt ¼" from

the binding's end. Lay the final end of the binding strip over it and mark with a pin the point where this strip meets the pin at the end of the first strip.

I always position this pin to follow the angle at the end of the first strip. This pin marks the seam line joining the two strip ends. Unfold and trim the end strip ¼" outside the pin at a 45° angle. Trim the point. Pin the two binding strip ends together and stitch with a ¼" seam. Press the seam allowance open. Refold the binding in half lengthwise and pin it to the quilt. Stitch from the point where you left off to the starting point, back tacking at both ends.

Wrap the binding around the perimeter of the quilt to the back side as you stitch. Align the crease with the stitching line that attached the binding strip. Hem stitch by hand to secure the binding to the back of the quilt. At the corners, stitch to the end of the stitching line. Position the binding for the beginning of the next side. Take a stitch to secure the binding for the next side to the corner, and use your needle to tuck under the excess at the miter. Continue in this manner until the binding is hand stitched all around the quilt.

Pattern Ratings

One rotary cutter means the pattern's cutting involves nothing but squares, rectangles, half-square triangles, and quarter-square triangles.

Two cutters means the rotary cutting involves additional shapes.

One spool means that the sewing is very easy, with only squares and rectangles.

Two spools means the sewing is pretty easy, with basic stars and the like.

Three spools means set-in seams, lots of points, or small pieces.

One light bulb means easy thinking; you won't give your brain much of a workout.

Two bulbs means you will need to keep a few different kinds of blocks or units straight.

Three bulbs means you'll need to keep your head screwed on straight and follow the diagrams carefully.

*+@ Do You Get My Meaning?

No, these are not expletives. They are simply a short way to refer to something in the pattern. These terms are defined below, in no particular order (I couldn't figure out how to alphabetize symbols!).

+ The + symbol indicates a measurement in sixteenths of inches. Simply add ¹⁄₁₆" to the listed number. Because sixteenths are not on most rotary rulers, you may need to find the line corresponding to the listed measurement and go halfway to the next higher ⅛".

● Set-in seams (or Y seams) are indicated by this symbol. Stitch only to the dot, not to the raw edge.

●----Partial seams are indicated by this pink dot and line symbol.

@ means "at." It indicates that the number of borders, sashes, or backing panels listed should be cut in the dimensions that follow.

*+@ Do You Get My Meaning? continued

A refers to the A patch.

(A) indicates that the A patch has already been sewn in a previous step. Just add the lettered patch outlined in black to the unit already made.

U1 refers to Unit 1.

} U1 indicates that bracketed elements are the patches previously assembled for Unit 1.

X refers to the X block.

fat qtrs. means fat quarters, equivalent to ¼ yard of fabric cut 18" x 22" instead of 9" x 44".

Cut Size or Finished?

Any question you may have about dimensions or quantities is addressed here.

All patch cutting dimensions include ¼" seam allowances.

Listed block sizes are finished sizes. That means the blocks would be ½" larger than the listed size if you were to measure from raw edge to raw edge.

Some blocks have finished sizes such as 12⅜" or 8½". I made them these sizes to make rotary cutting of their patches more accurate.

Templates are drafted with mathematical precision; rotary cutting dimensions are rounded to the nearest ¹⁄₁₆". In fact, almost all of the rotary cutting dimensions in the book are accurate to within ²⁄₁₀₀ of an inch.

Block and patch cutting dimensions do not include extra for trimming down or squaring up blocks.

Border lengths are exact with seam allowances included. If desired, cut them a little longer to be safe.

Borders cut from yardage are assumed to be seamless. Borders cut from fat quarters are not. This accounts for the discrepancy in fabric requirements for yardage and fat quarters.

Cut Size or Finished? continued

Backing dimensions allow for ¼" seam allowances between panels and 8" of extra length and width for easy mounting on long-arm quilting machines. For some of the rectangular quilts, backing measurements are for panels seamed together crosswise in order to conserve yardage.

All strips are cut on the lengthwise grain. They are 18" long unless marked by *. These shorter strips make your scrap quilt as scrappy as possible.

Some Strips (marked by *) are 19" long in order to better fit long patches. These strips are called for only when yardage rather than fat quarters is indicated.

Some strips (as indicated by *) need to be cut into patches of more than one length to conserve yardage.

Trapezoids' lengths are such that you should cut off one corner at a 45° angle.

Diamonds' cutting dimensions are measured from side to side, not point to corner.

Some patterns could easily be made from strip piecing using the given patch dimensions for strip widths and later cuts. However, my instructions are for rotary-cut patches (or templates if you prefer) in order to maximize the scrappy quality of the quilts.

The number of strips in the cutting chart assumes the strip width is the smaller dimension in the case of rectangular patches. The long side of the rectangle will be on the lengthwise grain.

The number of fat quarters listed is the minimum fabric requirement. The photographed quilts were made from my stash, and small portions of many fat quarters were used. If you do not have a stash, you may want to buy more fat quarters than the listed number in order to achieve a look that is as scrappy as the example.

More than Meets the Eye

The diagrams actually tell you more than you may think. Once you know all that the pictures convey, you may find that you don't even need to read the instructions!

Patches that are closer together in the block piecing diagram are joined first. Only the first patches to be stitched are touching in the upper left corner. Lower in the block diagram (and often to the right as well), you will see more and more patches joined. For a clear picture of the sewing sequence, first look at the top of the diagram; for later steps, look at the lower parts of the diagram.

In the diagrams, elements that were stitched together previously are indicated with lines around the unit, but not between its patches.

A few patterns are presented with pictures showing a patch added in each step. The patch to add is lettered and outlined in black to make it stand out from parts sewn previously.

Templates show grainline, patch letter used in diagrams and charts, seamline, cutting line, point trims, and rotary cutting dimensions. You can also use the templates to check the accuracy of your rotary cutting.

Miscellaneous Tips

For some quilts, especially those you want to make with a block-by-block plan, you may need to cut sets of matching patches. Be sure to account for this in your rotary cutting.

"Another Look" photographs show quilts that differ in colors, styles, and sometimes sizes from the patterns. Some require only simple color substitutions; others may change the yardage amounts and patch counts.

For the sake of brevity, fabrics may be called "blue" when they actually include neighboring hues such as turquoise and purple.

Make a test block before cutting up your fabric. This will help you perfect your technique and work out the contrasts. This may also point out errors in your cutting, sewing, or understanding.

Rotary Cutting Patches

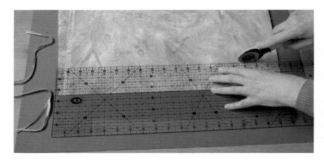

Strips. *Trim off selvages. Stack 4 fat quarters, aligning trimmed long sides. If they vary in length, arrange fabrics with short sides even on one end. Press the stack. Trim ⅛" from the trimmed edge to assure that all 4 strips will be the same width. Trim the aligned short side at right angles to the freshly trimmed long side to square it up. Lay your rotary ruler over the stack, aligning the listed rule line with the trimmed long edge. Cut along the edge of the ruler to make a strip.*

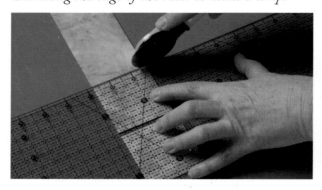

Squares and Rectangles. *Lay your ruler over the trimmed short side of the strip, with the listed rule line aligned with the edge of the fabric stack. Cut along the ruler's edge to complete a square or rectangle. Continue cutting additional squares or rectangles from the strip in the same way.*

Quarter-Square Triangles. *Start by cutting squares and cutting the squares into half-square triangles. Do not move the triangles; leave them arranged in a square. Lay your ruler along the uncut diagonal of the stack of 4 squares. The edge of the ruler should run exactly from corner to corner. Cut along the edge of the ruler to complete 4 stacks of triangles.*

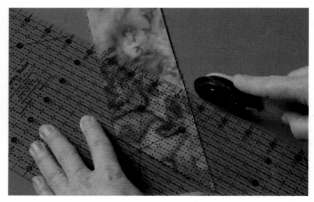

Diamonds. *Lay the 45° line of your ruler over the long side of the strip and cut off a triangle from one corner of the strip. Lay your ruler over this angled edge of the strip, with the listed rule line aligned with the edge of the strip. Cut along the ruler's edge to complete a diamond. Continue cutting diamonds this way from the rest of the strip.*

Half-Square Triangles (left). *Start by cutting squares. Lay your ruler diagonally over a stack of 4 squares. The edge of the ruler should run exactly from corner to corner of the squares. Cut along the edge of the ruler to make two stacks of triangles.*

Three of a Kind

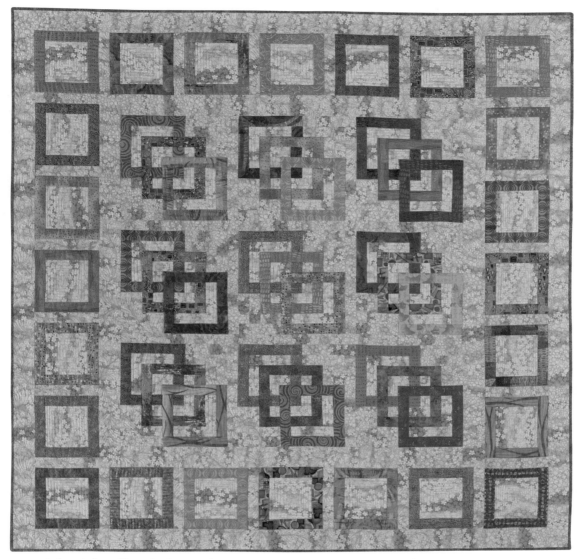

52" x 52" wall quilt designed and pieced by Judy Martin; quilted by Nichole Webb. One, two, or three rings are made from each bright contemporary fabric in this quilt. All rings contrast with a single Japanese-style background fabric. The rings appear to float over the background, although they are actually pieced in.

I started with a half dozen fat quarters of contemporary fabrics and drew the color scheme of red orange, yellow green, and blue green from them. A search of my stash yielded few appropriate partners, so I made a trip to my local quilt shop. (Actually, I make a trip to the quilt shop before starting any of my quilts.) Knowing that I probably wouldn't make a second quilt with these fabrics, I purchased fat quarters. By piecing the backing from leftovers, I used up most of the fat quarters that I included in the quilt.

A pieced backing might make hand quilting more difficult because of the extra thickness of the seam allowances. This is not a problem for machine quilting, however. If you want to piece your backing from leftovers, it will add to the variety of scraps. Simply add the backing yardage (multiplying by 4 to convert to fat quarters) to the fat quarters for the quilt top.

Yardage and Dimensions for Various Quilt Sizes

Yardage	Queen	Twin	Wall
Cream Print **Various Brights** **Binding** **Backing**	7½ yds./30 fat qtrs. 4½ yds./18 fat qtrs. ¾ yd. 8¾ yds.	6¼ yds./25 fat qtrs. 3½ yds./14 fat qtrs. ¾ yd. 6 yds.	3 yds./12 fat qtrs. 1¾ yds./7 fat qtrs. ½ yd. 3½ yds.
Quilt Dimensions **Block Size** **Number of Blocks**	92" x 92" 10" 36 blocks set 6 x 6	71" x 92" 10" 24 blocks set 4 x 6	52" x 52" 10" 9 blocks set 3 x 3

Cutting Requirements for Various Quilt Sizes

Fabric	Queen #18" Strips #borders	Queen #Patches border size	Twin #18" Strips # borders	Twin #Patches border size	Wall #18" Strips #borders	Wall #Patches border size
Cream Print						
Border	2 @	1½" x 92½"	2 @	1½" x 90½"	2 @	2½" x 52½"
Border	2 @	1½" x 90½"	2 @	1½" x 71½"	2 @	2½" x 48½"
Border	2 @	7" x 78½"	2 @	7½" x 65½"	2 @	2½" x 36½"
Border	2 @	7" x 65½"	2 @	7" x 57½"	2 @	2½" x 32½"
Long sashes	5 @	1½" x 65½"	5 @	1½" x 43½"	2 @	1½" x 32½"
4½" x 4½"	16	48 G	14	42 G	8	24 G
1½" x 10½"	30*	30 H	18*	18 H	6*	6 H
1½" x 6½"	24	48 F	21	42 F	12	24 F
1½" x 4½"	38*	144 D	26*	96 D	10*	36 D
1½" x 3½"	54	216 C	36	144 C	14	54 C
1½" x 2½"	24	144 B	16	96 B	6	36 B
1½" x 1½"	11*	144 A	8*	96 A	3*	36 A
Bright Prints						
1½" x 6½"	60	120 F	45	90 F	21	42 F
1½" x 5½"	92	276 E	68	204 E	31	93 E
1½" x 4½"	28	84 D	22	66 D	11	33 D
1½" x 3½"	9	36 C	6	24 C	3	9 C
1½" x 2½"	12	72 B	8	48 B	3	18 B
1½" x 1½"	20	216 A	14	144 A	5	54 A
Binding		2" x 385"		2" x 340"		2" x 225"
Backing	3 panels @	34" x 100"	2 panels @	40" x 100"	2 panels @	30½" x 60"

To conserve fabric, cut 1 D and 1 A in the same strip as 1 H. The number of strips of A and D has been reduced accordingly.

To match patches within a ring, as I did, cut brights in matched sets of 1 D, 2 E, and 1 F; 1 A, 2 B, 1 C, and 2 E; and 5 A, 1 E, and 1 F.

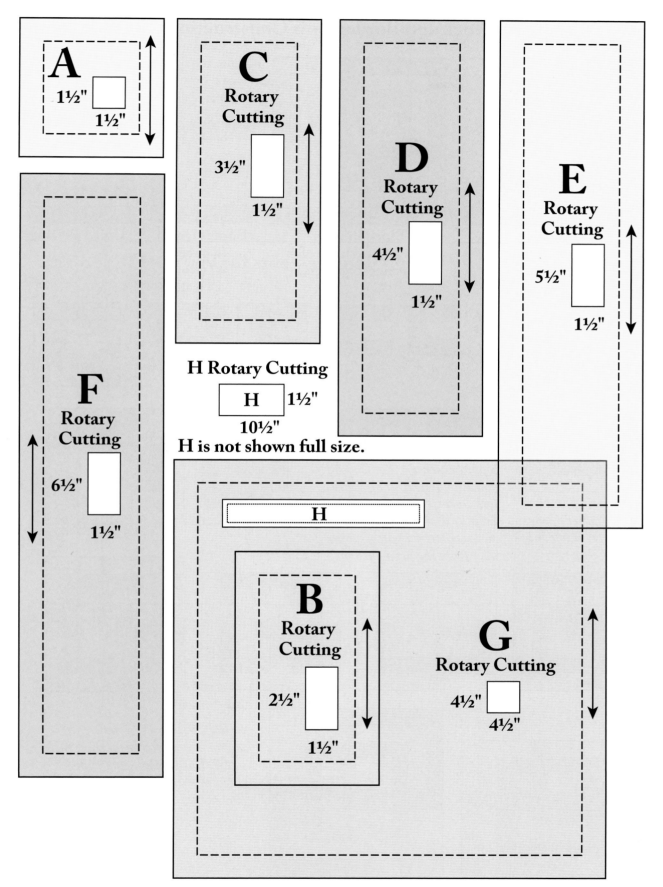

A

1½"

1½"

C

Rotary
Cutting

3½"

1½"

D

Rotary
Cutting

4½"

1½"

E

Rotary
Cutting

5½"

1½"

H Rotary Cutting

H   1½"

10½"

H is not shown full size.

F

Rotary
Cutting

6½"

1½"

H

B

Rotary
Cutting

2½"

1½"

G

Rotary Cutting

4½"

4½"

27

Block and Border Unit Construction

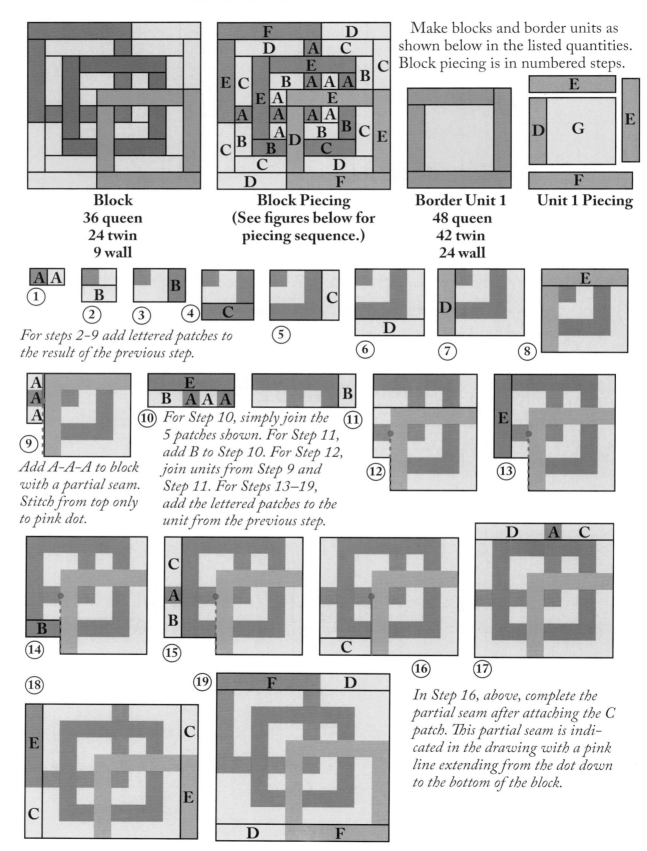

Make blocks and border units as shown below in the listed quantities. Block piecing is in numbered steps.

Block
36 queen
24 twin
9 wall

Block Piecing
(See figures below for piecing sequence.)

Border Unit 1
48 queen
42 twin
24 wall

Unit 1 Piecing

For steps 2–9 add lettered patches to the result of the previous step.

Add A-A-A to block with a partial seam. Stitch from top only to pink dot.

For Step 10, simply join the 5 patches shown. For Step 11, add B to Step 10. For Step 12, join units from Step 9 and Step 11. For Steps 13–19, add the lettered patches to the unit from the previous step.

In Step 16, above, complete the partial seam after attaching the C patch. This partial seam is indicated in the drawing with a pink line extending from the dot down to the bottom of the block.

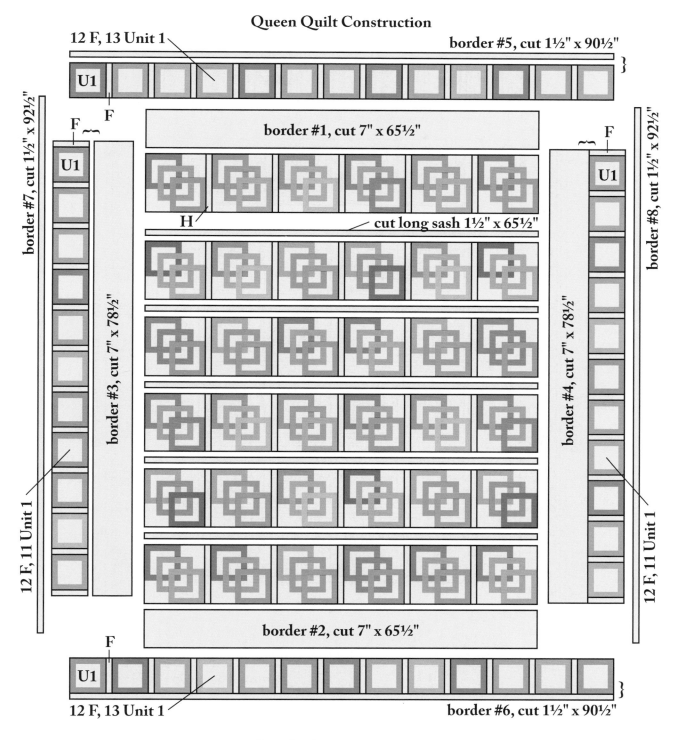

Queen Quilt Construction

12 F, 13 Unit 1

border #5, cut 1½" x 90½"

U1

border #7, cut 1½" x 92½"

F ~~ F

U1

border #3, cut 7" x 78½"

border #1, cut 7" x 65½"

H

cut long sash 1½" x 65½"

12 F, 11 Unit 1

border #2, cut 7" x 65½"

F

U1

12 F, 13 Unit 1

border #6, cut 1½" x 90½"

~~ F

U1

border #8, cut 1½" x 92½"

border #4, cut 7" x 78½"

12 F, 11 Unit 1

Quilt Construction

Referring to the the diagram for your quilt size, make rows by joining blocks with H rectangles between them. Stitch each row but the bottom one to a long, narrow sash. Join all rows, including the bottom one. You should have sashes between all block rows.

To make the pieced borders, join Unit 1's with cream F rectangles between them. Sew these pieced borders to plain borders where indicated by brackets in the quilt diagram. Pin and stitch borders to the quilt in numerical order as shown in the quilt diagram.

Twin Quilt Construction

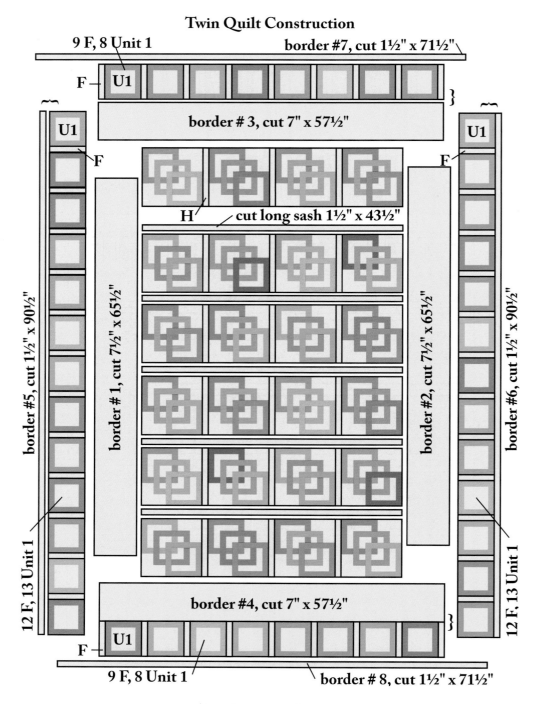

9 F, 8 Unit 1

border #7, cut 1½" x 71½"

F — U1

U1

F

border #3, cut 7" x 57½"

H

cut long sash 1½" x 43½"

border #5, cut 1½" x 90½"

border #1, cut 7½" x 65½"

border #2, cut 7½" x 65½"

border #6, cut 1½" x 90½"

12 F, 13 Unit 1

12 F, 13 Unit 1

border #4, cut 7" x 57½"

F — U1

9 F, 8 Unit 1

border # 8, cut 1½" x 71½"

Quilt Finishing

Trim off selvages and square up the backing fabric. Cut out backing panels in the size and quantity listed in the cutting chart. Pin and seam together the backing panels.

At this point, you may send out the top for quilting. If you will be hand or machine quilting it yourself, plan the quilting and mark it at this time. For my quilt, Nichole Webb machine quilted in the ditch around the boxes; she quilted a pattern of feathers and bubbles in the background. After you mark any quilting, lay the backing face down, and center the batting and the quilt top, face up, over it. Thread baste or pin baste with safety pins, trying to avoid the path of your planned quilting. Quilt, remove markings, and bind to finish.

Wall Quilt Construction

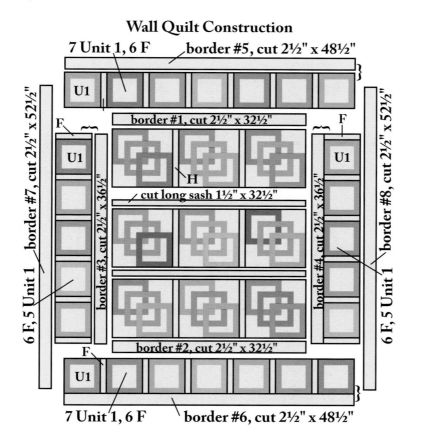

7 Unit 1, 6 F   border #5, cut 2½" x 48½"

border #7, cut 2½" x 52½"

6 F, 5 Unit 1

U1

F

border #1, cut 2½" x 32½"

H

cut long sash 1½" x 32½"

border #3, cut 2½" x 36½"

border #4, cut 2½" x 36½"

border #2, cut 2½" x 32½"

F

U1

F

U1

border #8, cut 2½" x 52½"

6 F, 5 Unit 1

7 Unit 1, 6 F   border #6, cut 2½" x 48½"

Flower Child

52¾" square wall quilt designed and pieced by Judy Martin; quilted by Linda V. Taylor. This quilt was made in a paint-by-number scheme, with blue background patches and green leaves, stems, and border triangles. However, the flower color ranges from yellow through orange and on to hot pink. This variability takes the color plan from predictable to delightfully surprising. The shifting of color within a single flower adds punch. I placed flower colors to blend with neighboring diamonds in some areas and contrast in others. The blues and greens are more uniform in color and value, and serve to calm this bright quilt to a manageable level. Batiks and contemporary fabrics with a mostly solid look set the style.

Yardage, Dimensions, & Number of Blocks for Various Quilt Sizes

Yardage	Queen	Twin	Wall
Bright Green Prints **Light Blue Prints** **Warm Brights** **Binding** **Backing**	3½ yds./14 fat qtrs. 7½ yds./30 fat qtrs. 4½ yds./18 fat qtrs. ¾ yds. 9⅜ yds.	3 yds./12 fat qtrs. 5 yds./20 fat qtrs. 3 yds./12 fat qtrs. ¾ yd. 7⅝ yds.	¾ yd./3 fat qtrs. 2½ yds./10 fat qtrs. 1¾ yds./7 fat qtrs. ½ yd. 3⅝ yds.
Quilt Dimensions **Block Size** **Number of Blocks**	99" x 99" 12⅜" 36 blks. set 6 x 6	77¾" x 90⅜" 12⅜" 20 blks. set 4 x 5	52¾" x 52¾" 12⅜" 9 blks. set 3 x 3

Cutting Requirements for Various Quilt Sizes

Fabric	Queen #18" Strips #borders	Queen #Patches border size	Twin #18" Strips #borders	Twin #Patches border size	Wall #18" Strips #borders	Wall #Patches border size
Bright Greens						
Borders	2 @	4½" x 99½ "	2 @	4½" x 82⅞"		
Borders	2 @	4½" x 91½"	2 @	4½" x 78¼"		
3⅞" x 3⅞"	1	8 B	1	8 B	1	8 B
3" x 3"	16	160 C	14	132 C	9	88 C
2⅝" x 2⅝"	24	72 A	14	40 A	6	18 A
¾" x 11"	36	36 F	20	20 F	9	9 F
Lt. Blue Prints						
Borders	2 @	3¾" x 81¼"	2 @	5½" x 62⅜"	2 @	3⅛+" x 43"
Borders	2 @	3¾" x 74¾"	2 @	5⅝" x 60"	2 @	3⅛+" x 37⅝"
6" x 6"	18	72 E	10	40 E	5	18 E
3⅞" x 3⅞"	36	288 B	20	160 B	9	72 B
3" x 3"	44	440 C	29	284 C	16	152 C
2⅝" x 5⅝"	24	72 D	14	40 D	6	18 D
Warm Brights						
2⅝" x 2⅝"	126	376 A	84	252 A	48	142 A
Binding		2" x 410"		2" x 350"		2" x 225"
Backing	3 panels @	36½" x 107"	3 panels @	33½" x 86"	2 panels @	31" x 61"

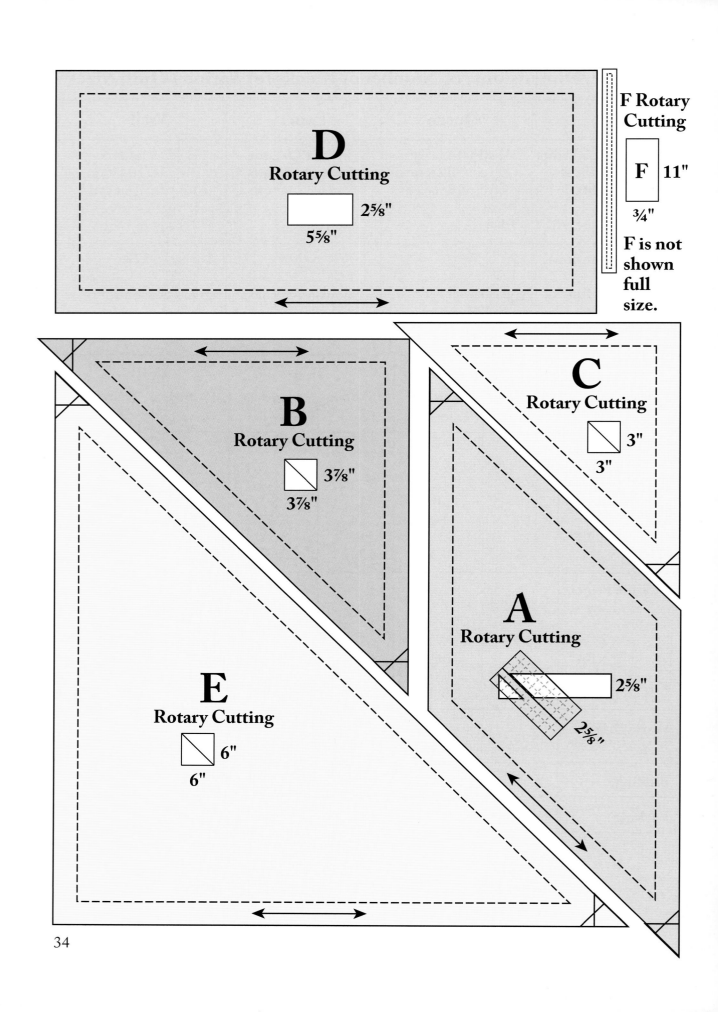

D
Rotary Cutting

2⅝"
5⅝"

F Rotary Cutting

F 11"

¾"

F is not shown full size.

B
Rotary Cutting

3⅞"
3⅞"

C
Rotary Cutting

3"
3"

E
Rotary Cutting

6"
6"

A
Rotary Cutting

2⅝"
2⅝"

Block
36 queen
20 twin
9 wall

Block Piecing

Block Construction

Trim points of diamonds and triangles before piecing to help with patch alignment. Sew a C and a B to each A. Note that C's and B's go in different positions in the various flower and leaf sections. Press seam allowances away from leaves. In the flower sections, press all seam allowances clockwise. Add an E to each leaf section, pressing seams toward E. Add stems as shown below left. Join flower sections in pairs to make squares. Press seam allowances clockwise. Add D to two of the squares as shown in the block diagram. Sew one of these to the leaf section, pressing seams away from leaves. Sew the other D section to the remaining flower section, pressing seams clockwise. Join half blocks to complete the block. Make the quantity listed.

Unit 1
76 queen
62 twin
40 wall

Unit 2
76 queen
62 twin
40 wall

Unit 3
4 queen
4 twin
4 wall

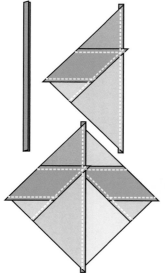

Stem Piecing
Fold the F rectangle in half lengthwise with right sides out. Insert folded F between two C-A-B-E segments, aligning all 4 raw edges. Stitch; press seam allowances away from the stem. Trim off stem ends even with neighboring patches.

Twin Quilt Construction Diagram

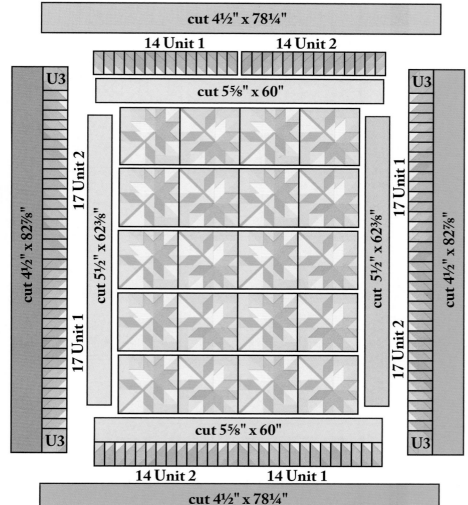

cut 4½" x 78¼"

14 Unit 1   **14 Unit 2**

cut 5⅝" x 60"

U3   U3

17 Unit 2   17 Unit 1

cut 4½" x 82⅞"   cut 5½" x 62⅜"   cut 5½" x 62⅜"   cut 4½" x 82⅞"

17 Unit 1   17 Unit 2

U3   U3

cut 5⅝" x 60"

14 Unit 2   **14 Unit 1**

cut 4½" x 78¼"

Border and Quilt Construction

See the border unit diagrams below the block diagrams. Make the number of units listed for your quilt size. Refer to the quilt diagram for your quilt size, here or on the previous page. Join border units as shown.

Arrange blocks, turning them as you wish. Join blocks in rows as shown in the quilt diagrams. Press seams to the left in one row and to the right in the next. Join rows, pressing seams to one side.

Add borders. Press quilt top. Layer, baste, quilt, and bind to finish.

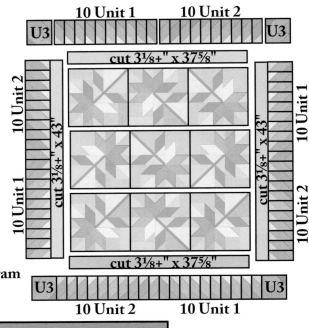

Wall Quilt Construction Diagram

Queen Quilt Construction Diagram

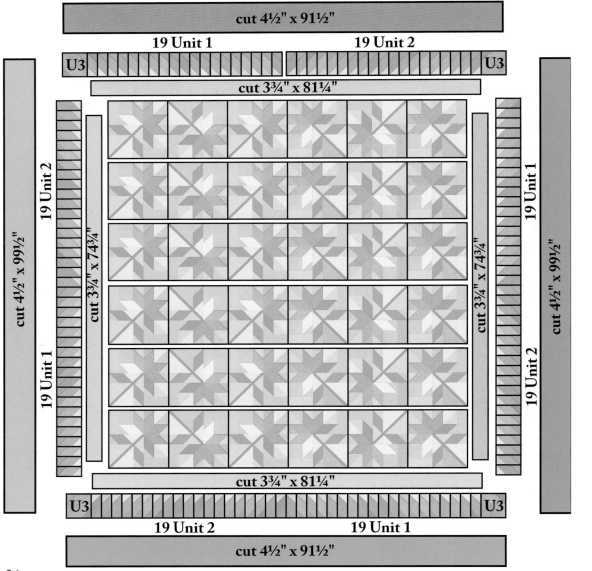

Monet's Wedding Ring

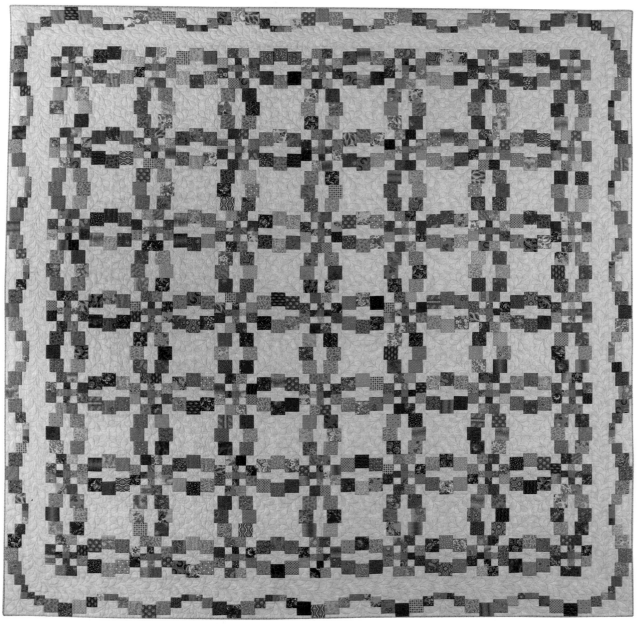

90" x 90" queen-sized quilt designed and pieced by Judy Martin; quilted by Kathy Olson. Lots of mid-size florals and late-19th Century reproductions are featured in this darker version of a 1930s multi-color pastel color scheme. A mottled neutral background stands in for the more usual muslin. Rose, green, blue, yellow, and purple are included, along with small touches of soft brown.

This quilt is a good one for busy prints. It is not important to distinguish individual patches here. The secondary pattern of rings is more important.

This calls for a swath of color. I like the effect of patches blending with neighbors in some places and standing apart in others. With pastels (even darkish ones), values can be very even. I like to spice things up a bit by including a few deep darks and some lighter prints along with the pastels.

The curves are less obvious here than in a Double Wedding Ring. I liken them to an Impressionist painting. Some distance helps to see the rings. I named the quilt to acknowledge the traditional quilt and the Impressionist painter.

Yardage and Dimensions for Various Quilt Sizes

Yardage	Queen	Twin	Baby
Lt. Cream Print **Medium Prints** **Dk. Pink Accent** **Binding** **Backing**	7¼ yds./29 fat qtrs. 4¾ yds./19 fat qtrs. ¼ yd./1 fat qtr. ¾ yd. 8⅝ yds.	5 yds./20 fat qtrs. 3¾ yds./15 fat qtrs. ¼ yd./1 fat qtr. ¾ yd. 5¾ yds.	2¾ yds./11 fat qtrs. 2 yds./8 fat qtrs. ¼ yd./1 fat qtr. ½ yd. 3⅝ yds.
Quilt Dimensions **Block Size** **Number of Blocks**	90" x 90" 6" 49 Y, 84 Z	66" x 90" 6" 35 Y, 58 Z	54" x 54" 6" 16 Y, 24 Z

Cutting Requirements for Various Quilt Sizes

Fabric	Queen #18" Strips #borders	Queen #Patches border size	Twin #18" Strips #borders	Twin #Patches border size	Baby #18" Strips #borders	Baby #Patches border size
Lt. Cream Print Borders		2 @ 3" x 83½" 2 @ 3" x 78½"		2 @ 3" x 78½" 2 @ 3" x 59½"		2 @ 3" x 47½" 2 @ 3" x 42½"
☐ 6½" x 6½"	18	36 F	12	24 F	5	9 F
☐ 3" x 3"	1	4 K	1	4 K	1	4 K
☐ 2" x 6½"	12	24 G	10	20 G	6	12 G
☐ 2" x 2"	26	204 B	19	148 B	9	72 B
☐ 1½" x 6½"	56	112 E	41	82 E	20	40 E
☐ 1½" x 3½"	6	24 I	5	20 I	3	12 I
☐ 1½" x 3"	4	16 J	4	16 J	4	16 J
☐ 1½" x 1½"	18	196 A	13	140 A	6	64 A
☐ 1" x 2½"	98	588 D	70	420 D	32	192 D
☐ 1" x 2"	7	56 H	6	48 H	4	32 H
Medium Prints						
☐ 2½" x 2½"	98	588 C	70	420 C	32	192 C
☐ 2" x 2"	56	448 B	41	328 B	20	160 B
☐ 1½" x 1½"	23	252 A	18	188 A	9	96 A
Dk. Pink Accent						
☐ 1½" x 1½"	7	77 A	6	59 A	3	32 A
Binding		2" x 375"		2" x 330"		2" x 230"
Backing	3 panels @	33¼" x 98"	2 panels @	37½" x 98"	2 panels @	31¼" x 62"

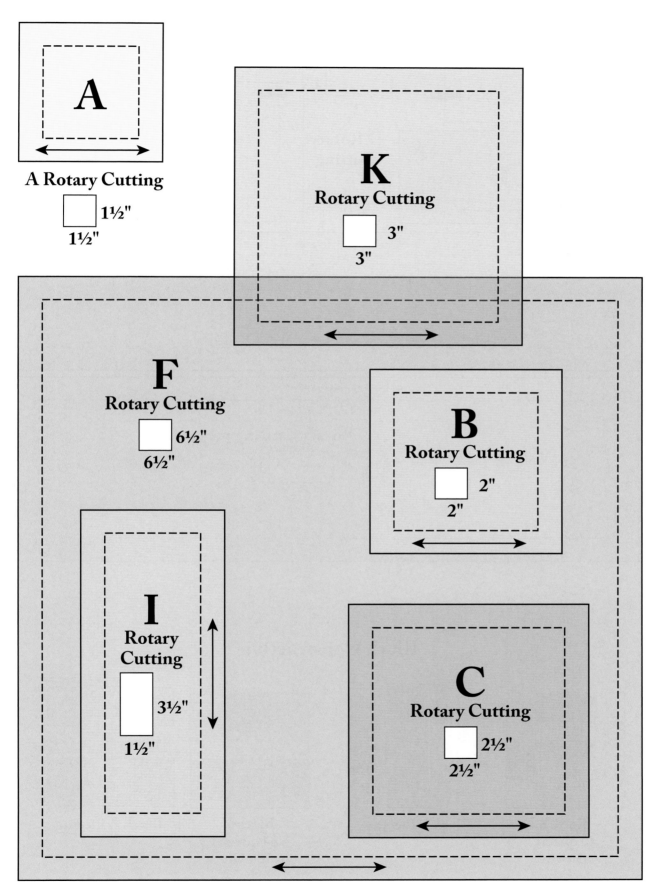

A

A Rotary Cutting

1½"
1½"

K
Rotary Cutting

3"
3"

F
Rotary Cutting

6½"
6½"

B
Rotary Cutting

2"
2"

I
Rotary
Cutting

3½"
1½"

C
Rotary Cutting

2½"
2½"

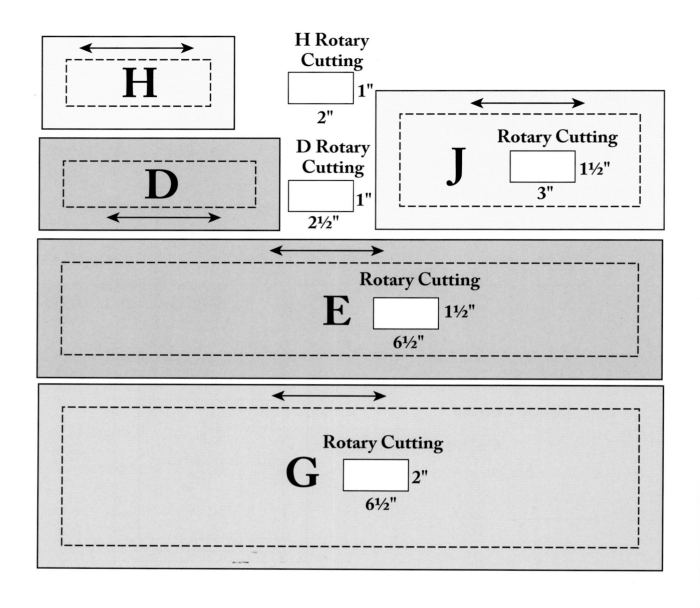

H Rotary Cutting
2" × 1"

D Rotary Cutting
2½" × 1"

J Rotary Cutting
3" × 1½"

E Rotary Cutting
6½" × 1½"

G Rotary Cutting
6½" × 2"

Block Construction

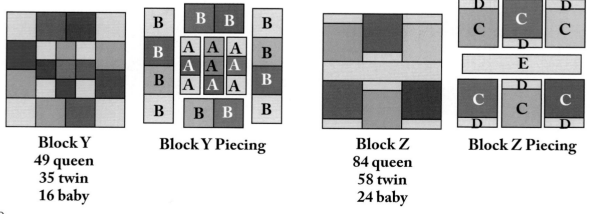

Block Y
49 queen
35 twin
16 baby

Block Y Piecing

Block Z
84 queen
58 twin
24 baby

Block Z Piecing

Border Unit Construction

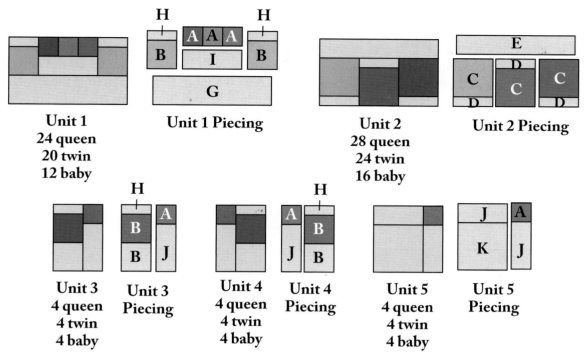

Unit 1
24 queen
20 twin
12 baby

Unit 1 Piecing

Unit 2
28 queen
24 twin
16 baby

Unit 2 Piecing

Unit 3
4 queen
4 twin
4 baby

Unit 3 Piecing

Unit 4
4 queen
4 twin
4 baby

Unit 4 Piecing

Unit 5
4 queen
4 twin
4 baby

Unit 5 Piecing

Make Units 1–5 as shown above. Press seams of Unit 1 away from H and accent colored A patches; press subsequent seams toward I, G, and the B ends of the unit. Press seams of Unit 2 away from D's and toward E. For Units 3 and 4 press seams toward dark squares; press the long seam toward the J side. For Unit 5, press seam allowances toward J's.

Block Construction

Join A and B squares as shown at left to make a Y block. Note that the center square is cut from the accent fabric. Press seam allowances within rows toward the dark fabrics; press long seams away from the center of the block. Make the number listed.

For Z, sew a light D to each of 6 C squares. Press seams toward C's. Join three of these, turning them as shown. Press seam allowances away from the center C. Repeat. Sew an E rectangle between C units as shown. Press seam allowances toward the E rectangle.

Baby Quilt Construction

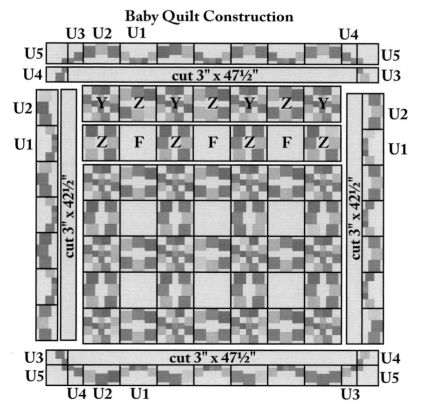

41

Quilt Construction

For this quilt, every second block is a Z block. Make Y-Z rows as shown in the diagram for your quilt size. Start and end each of these rows with a Y. Make Z block-F patch rows as well, starting and ending each of these rows with a Z. Within rows, press seam allowances away from Z blocks. Join rows, pressing seam allowances toward the Z-F rows.

Make pieced borders as shown in the quilt diagrams that follow, alternating Unit 1's and Unit 2's. Referring to the quilt construction diagrams, add Units 3, 4, and 5 to the ends of borders where indicated. Pin and then stitch plain and pieced borders to the quilt according to the diagram, attaching the borders having Unit 5's on the ends last.

Queen Quilt Construction

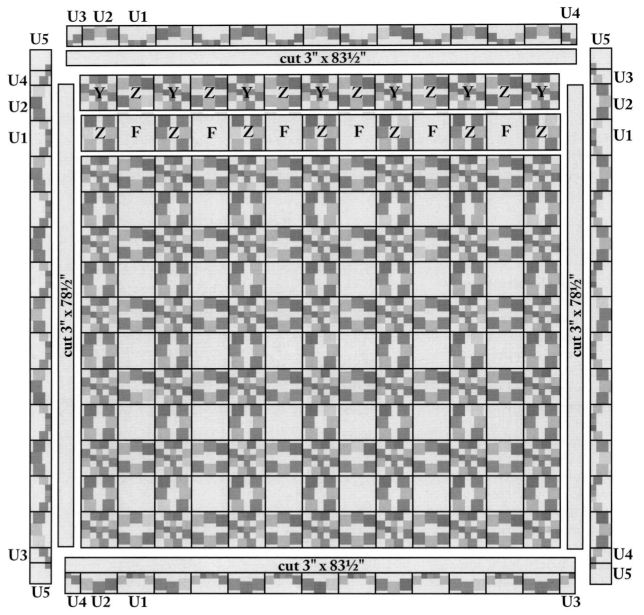

Quilt Finishing

Prewash and press the backing fabric. Trim off selvages and square up the fabric. Cut out backing panels in the size and quantity listed in the cutting chart. Pin and seam together the backing panels.

At this point, you may send out the top for quilting. If you will be hand or machine quilting it yourself, plan the quilting and mark it if necessary. Kathy Olson machine quilted my Monet's Wedding Ring with freehand feathers in the plain areas.

Unless your quilting frame has rollers for batting and backing, you will need to baste the layers. Lay the backing face down and center the batting and the quilt top, face up, over it. Baste with thread or safety pins, trying to avoid the path of your planned quilting. Quilt, remove any markings, and bind to finish.

Twin Quilt Construction

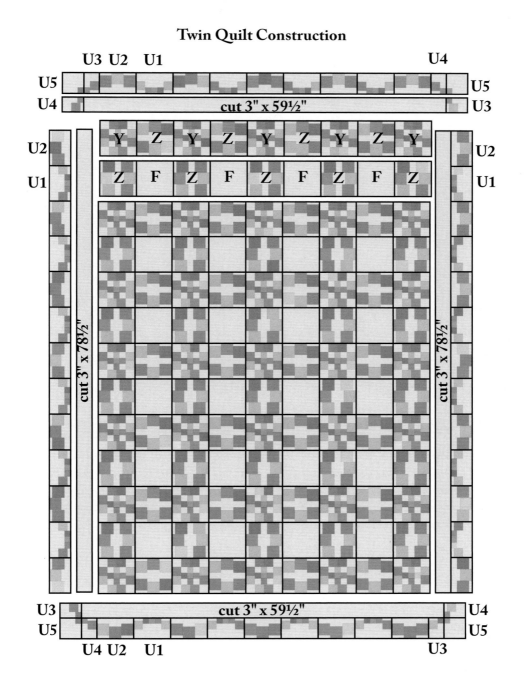

Another Look: Monet's Wedding Ring

Designed by Judy Martin; pieced by Chris Hulin; quilted by Jean Nolte. The quilt shown here is owned by Jennifer and Scott Thompson. Bright batiks on a contemporary sky blue background give a fresh new style to this variation of a traditional Wedding Ring. Scraps of blues, greens, and purples have a cool tranquility that juxtaposes nicely with the hot pink accents.

Meteor Shower

54½" square wall quilt designed by Judy Martin; made by Margy Sieck. The name for this quilt was chosen by polling readers like you on my web site. I often invite you to share your opinions in this way. I also invite you to share pictures of the quilts you have made from my patterns. To view photos, vote in a poll, or download a free Block of the Moment, go to http://www.judymartin.com.

Margy featured two contrasting star colors in each of the four blocks. After arranging the blocks, she made the border blocks in colors to match the neighboring block. For added interest, bright, dark, and pastel batiks provide areas of high contrast as well as those of low contrast. Margy selected many scraps of each color from her stash in order to get the variability that makes the stars sparkle.

Yardage, Dimensions, & Number of Blocks for Various Quilt Sizes

Yardage	Queen	Twin	Wall
Purple (for Border)	3 yds./6 fat qtrs.	2¾ yds./5 fat qtrs.	
Cream (for Border)	3⅜ yds./16 fat qtrs.	2⅞ yds./14 fat qtrs.	
Cream Prints	5¼ yds./21 fat qtrs.	4¼ yds./17 fat qtrs.	2½ yds./10 fat qtrs.
Bright Oranges	1½ yds./6 fat qtrs.	1¼ yds./5 fat qtrs.	¾ yd./3 fat qtrs.
Pastel Oranges	¾ yd./3 fat qtrs.	½ yd./2 fat qtrs.	¼ yd./1 fat qtr.
Bright Blues	¾ yd./3 fat qtrs.	¾ yd./3 fat qtrs.	½ yd./2 fat qtrs.
Pastel Blues	¼ yd./1 fat qtr.	¼ yd./1 fat qtr.	¼ yd./1 fat qtr.
Bright Purples	1¼ yds./5 fat qtrs.	1 yd./4 fat qtrs.	¾ yd./3 fat qtrs.
Pastel Purples	½ yd./2 fat qtrs.	¼ yd./1 fat qtr.	¼ yd./1 fat qtr.
Bright Pinks	1¼ yds./5 fat qtrs.	¾ yd./3 fat qtrs.	¾ yd./3 fat qtrs.
Pastel Pinks	½ yd./2 fat qtr.	¼ yd./1 fat qtr.	¼ yd./1 fat qtr.
Bright Greens	¾ yd./3 fat qtrs.	¾ yd./3 fat qtrs.	½ yd./2 fat qtrs.
Pastel Greens	½ yd./2 fat qtr.	¼ yd./1 fat qtr.	¼ yd./1 fat qtr.
Binding	¾ yd.	¾ yd.	½ yd.
Backing	9⅝ yds.	8 yds.	3¾ yds.
Quilt Dimensions	100¾" x 100¾"	82" x 100¾"	54½" x 54½"
Block Sizes	18¾", 8½"	18¾", 8½"	18¾", 8½"
Number of Blocks	13 large, 24 small	10 large, 20 small	4 large, 20 small
Set	3 x 3	2 x 3	2 x 2

Cutting Requirements for Various Quilt Sizes

Fabric	Queen #18" Strips # borders	Queen #Patches border size	Twin #18" Strips # borders	Twin #Patches border size	Wall #18" Strips # borders	Wall #Patches border size
Purple (Border)						
Borders	2 @	4" x 101¼"	2 @	4" x 94¼"		
Borders	2 @	4" x 94¼"	2 @	4" x 82½"		
Cream (Border)						
Borders	4 @	10¾" x 56¾"	2 @	10¾" x 56¾"		
Borders			2 @	10¾" x 38"		
Cream						
◻ 5⅛" x 5⅛"	5	26 D	4	20 D	2	8 D
◻ 3⅞" x 3⅞"	7	52 C	5	40 C	2	16 C
◻ 3⅜" x 3⅜"	48	478 E	38	380 E	25	248 E
◻ 2⅝" x 2⅝"	40	478 G	32	380 G	21	248 G
▭ 2¼" x 4¾"	17	50 F	14	40 F	8	24 F
Bright Oranges						
◇ 2¼" x 2¼"	22	88 B	16	64 B	7	28 B
◇ 2" x 2"	29	144 A	26	128 A	10	48 A

Cutting Requirements for Various Quilt Sizes, continued

Fabric	Queen		Twin		Wall	
	#18" Strips	#Patches	#18" Strips	#Patches	#18" Strips	#Patches
Pastel Oranges 2¼" x 2¼"	16	63 B	14	56 B	6	21 B
Bright Blues 2¼" x 2¼"	7	28 B	11	44 B	11	44 B
2" x 2"	10	48 A	10	48 A	4	16 A
Pastel Blues 2¼" x 2¼"	6	21 B	6	21 B	2	7 B
Bright Purples 2¼" x 2¼"	17	68 B	12	48 B	12	48 B
2" x 2"	20	96 A	13	64 A	7	32 A
Pastel Purples 2¼" x 2¼"	11	42 B	7	28 B	4	14 B
Bright Pinks 2¼" x 2¼"	21	84 B	11	44 B	13	52 B
2" x 2"	13	64 A	10	48 A	4	16 A
Pastel Pinks 2¼" x 2¼"	7	28 B	6	21 B	2	7 B
Bright Greens 2¼" x 2¼"	7	28 B	10	40 B	5	20 B
2" x 2"	13	64 A	7	32 A	4	16 A
Pastel Greens 2¼" x 2¼"	7	28 B	4	14 B	2	7 B
Binding		2" x 420"		2" x 380"		2" x 235"
Backing	3 panels @	37" x 109"	3 panels @	37" x 90"	2 panels @	31½" x 63"

Note that the colors and patches listed here may be arranged randomly in multi-colored blocks as shown in the twin diagram, or they may be arranged as in the photograph on page 45. If you don't have a stash, and you don't want leftover fabric, I suggest the twin color placement. (You can make any size of quilt in either color place-ment.) If you don't have a stash and want to use the color placement in the photo, you will need to buy additional fat quarters for variety in stars.

The yardage was figured with pastel B's in the 7-pointed stars in the large block and bright dia-monds (A and B) everywhere else. Still, you may mix brights and pastels, as Margy did.

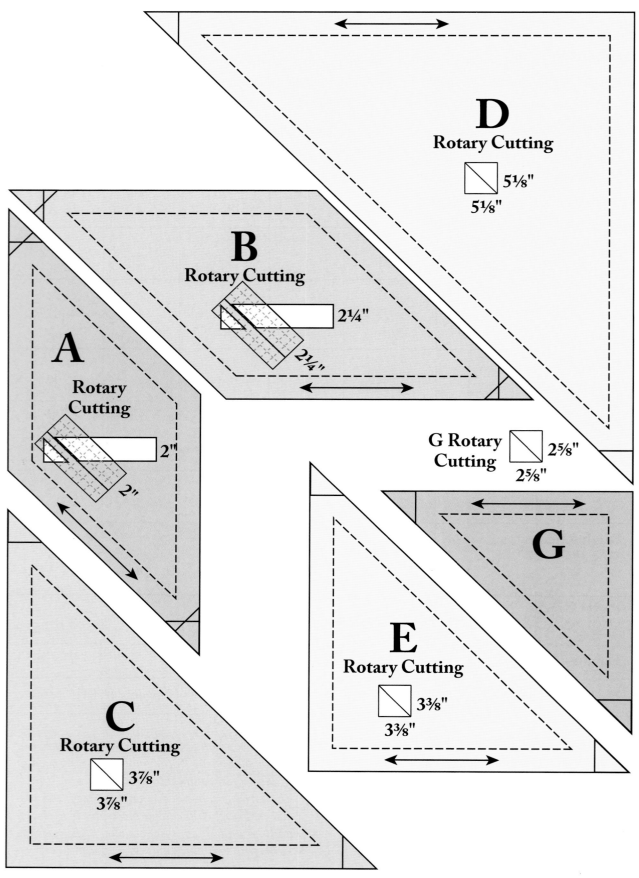

D
Rotary Cutting
5⅛"
5⅛"

B
Rotary Cutting
2¼"
2¼"

A
Rotary
Cutting
2"
2"

G Rotary
Cutting
2⅝"
2⅝"

G

E
Rotary Cutting
3⅜"
3⅜"

C
Rotary Cutting
3⅞"
3⅞"

Block Construction

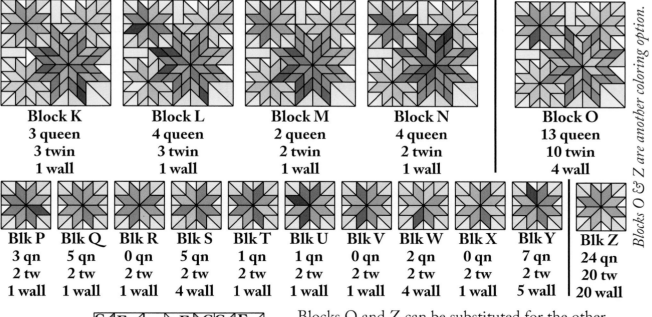

Block K	Block L	Block M	Block N	Block O
3 queen	4 queen	2 queen	4 queen	13 queen
3 twin	3 twin	2 twin	2 twin	10 twin
1 wall	1 wall	1 wall	1 wall	4 wall

Blk P	Blk Q	Blk R	Blk S	Blk T	Blk U	Blk V	Blk W	Blk X	Blk Y	Blk Z
3 qn	5 qn	0 qn	5 qn	1 qn	1 qn	0 qn	2 qn	0 qn	7 qn	24 qn
2 tw	2 tw	2 tw	2 tw	2 tw	2 tw	2 tw	2 tw	2 tw	2 tw	20 tw
1 wall	1 wall	1 wall	4 wall	1 wall	1 wall	1 wall	4 wall	1 wall	5 wall	20 wall

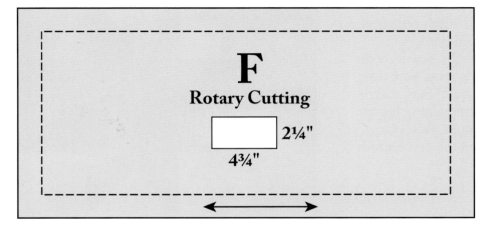

Piecing Blocks K–O **Piecing Blocks P–Z**

Blocks O and Z can be substituted for the other block colorings, if you prefer.

For this quilt, it is especially helpful to trim the points before stitching. Press all seam allowances clockwise to oppose at the centers of the stars.

For the small block, sew a G and an E to each B. Join two G-B-E parts to make each ¼-block square. Join quarters to make half blocks. Stitch across the center to complete the block. Make the quantity listed for your chosen quilt size.

Note that the 4 pink dots in the piecing diagram for Blocks K–O indicate set-in seams. (See page 18.) For the large blocks, join A's in 2 rows of 2 diamonds; join rows. Sew G's and E's to B diamonds. Arrange these parts, along with C, D, and F patches, as shown in the block piecing diagram. Stitch to complete the block. Make the listed number of blocks for the quilt in the size you have chosen.

F
Rotary Cutting

2¼"
4¾"

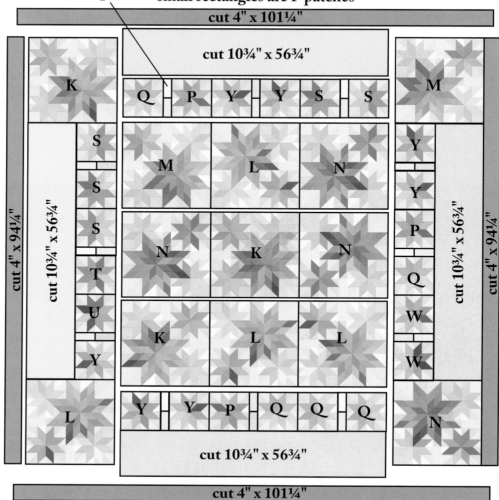

Queen Quilt Construction
small rectangles are F patches

F

cut 4" x 101¼"

cut 10¾" x 56¾"

| Q | P | Y | Y | S | S |

cut 4" x 94¼"   cut 10¾" x 56¾"

K		S	M
M	L	N	Y
			Y
N	K	N	P
			Q
K	L	L	W
			W
L			N

| Y | Y | P | Q | Q | Q |

cut 10¾" x 56¾"   cut 4" x 94¼"

cut 10¾" x 56¾"

cut 4" x 101¼"

Quilt Construction

Arrange blocks according to the diagram for your quilt size. Join the large blocks in the center of the quilt to make rows. Join rows. Join small blocks and F rectangles to make border strips as shown.

For the wall quilt, pin and stitch pieced side borders, then top and bottom borders.

For the twin and queen quilts, sew a cream border to each pieced border strip. Sew two of these to the sides of the quilt. Sew a large block to both ends of each remaining border. Sew to top and bottom of quilt. Add plain purple borders to sides, then top and bottom to complete the quilt top.

Right, 18¾" Meteor Shower block made by Judy Martin in 19th Century style scraps.

50

Another Look for Meteor Shower

Twin Quilt Construction
small rectangles are F patches

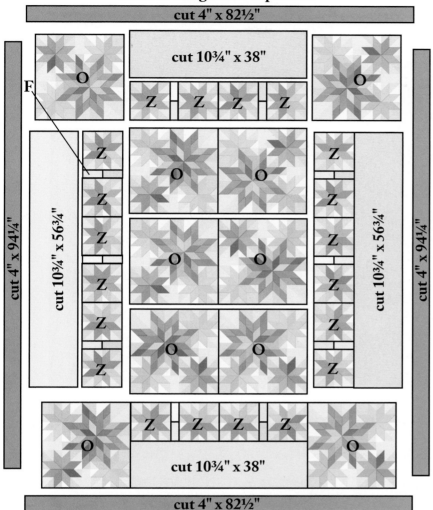

cut 4" x 82½"

cut 10¾" x 38"

O · F · O

Z Z Z Z

cut 4" x 94¼"

cut 10¾" x 56¾"

Z Z O O Z Z

Z Z O O Z Z

cut 10¾" x 56¾"

cut 4" x 94¼"

Z Z O O Z Z

O Z Z Z Z O

cut 10¾" x 38"

cut 4" x 82½"

Quilt Finishing

Prewash and press the backing fabric. Trim off the selvages, and square up the fabric. Cut out backing panels in the size and quantity listed in the cutting chart. Pin and seam together the backing panels.

At this point, you may send out the top to have it quilted. If you will be hand or machine quilting it yourself, plan the quilting and mark it if necessary. Margy Sieck machine quilted in the ditch around the stars and stippled the background of her Meteor Shower. Unless your quilting frame has rollers for the batting and backing, you will need to baste the layers. To baste, lay the backing face down, and center the batting and the quilt top, face up, over it. Thread baste or pin baste with safety pins, trying to avoid the path of your planned quilting. Quilt, remove any markings, and bind to finish.

Wall Quilt Construction
F small rectangles are F patches

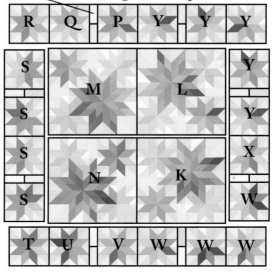

R Q P Y Y Y

S M L Y

S Y

S N K X

S W

T U V W W W

Rogue River Log Cabin

48" x 48" wall-size quilt designed and pieced by Judy Martin; quilted by Margy Sieck. Traditional-style prints as well as reproductions of 19th Century prints are featured in Rogue River Log Cabin.

Each block is made from 11 different scrap fabrics. I used my stash and cut just a couple of strips from each fabric. By cutting one strip into assorted patch lengths, starting with the longest, and fitting smaller patches into the leftovers, I was able to make the quilt as scrappy as possible.

This is a multi-colored quilt in a two-color plan. Fabrics are sorted into two types: light prints and dark prints. Here, the dark prints included red, pink, dark blue, dark green, and brown. Light prints included fabrics with cream, yellow, and light tan backgrounds. Some light prints have figures printed in dark colors. Nevertheless, they work as lights because they have more light than dark in them. Determine whether a print is light or dark by squinting at it or looking at it through a reducing glass.

Yardage and Dimensions for Various Quilt Sizes

Yardage	Queen	Twin	Wall
Dark Prints **Light Prints** **Binding** **Backing**	7½ yds./30 fat qtrs. 6¾ yds./27 fat qtrs. ¾ yd. 9⅛ yds.	5¾ yds./23 fat qtrs. 5 yds./20 fat qtrs. ¾ yd. 6⅛ yds.	2 yds./8 fat qtrs. 1¾ yds./7 fat qtrs. ½ yds 3⅜ yds.
Quilt Dimensions **Block Size** **Number of Blocks**	96" x 96" 6" 256 blocks set 16 x 16	72" x 96" 6" 192 blocks set 12 x 16	48" x 48" 6" 64 blocks set 8 x 8

 Cutting Requirements for Various Quilt Sizes

Fabric	Queen		Twin		Wall	
	#18" Strips	#Patches	#18" Strips	#Patches	#18" Strips	#Patches
Dark Prints ▢▭ 1½" x various	384	256 A–F	288	192 A–F	96	64 A–F
Light Prints ▢▭ 1½" x various	342	256 A–E	256	192 A–E	86	64 A–E
Binding		2" x 400"		2" x 350"		2" x 210"
Backing	3 panels @	35½" x 104"	2 panels @	40" x 104"	2 panels @	28¼" x 56"

Block Construction

Each block is scrappy, with six different dark prints and five different light prints per block. Note that patch letter A is for the smallest patch; B is 1" longer than A; C is 1" longer than B; and so on. Join all logs except F in pairs as follows: light A-dark E, light B-dark D, light C-dark C, light D-dark B, and light E-dark A. Press seam allowances toward dark.

Join one of each pair and one F patch to complete a block as shown below. Press seam allowances toward the F. Repeat to make the number of blocks listed for your quilt size.

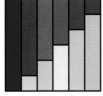

Block
256 queen
192 twin
64 wall

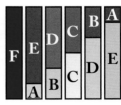

Block Piecing

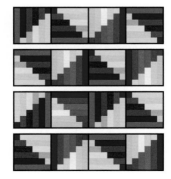

Star Piecing (at left)
9 queen
6 twin
1 wall
Use the blocks you have already made to make stars as follows: For each star, join 16 blocks in 4 rows of 4 each; join rows.

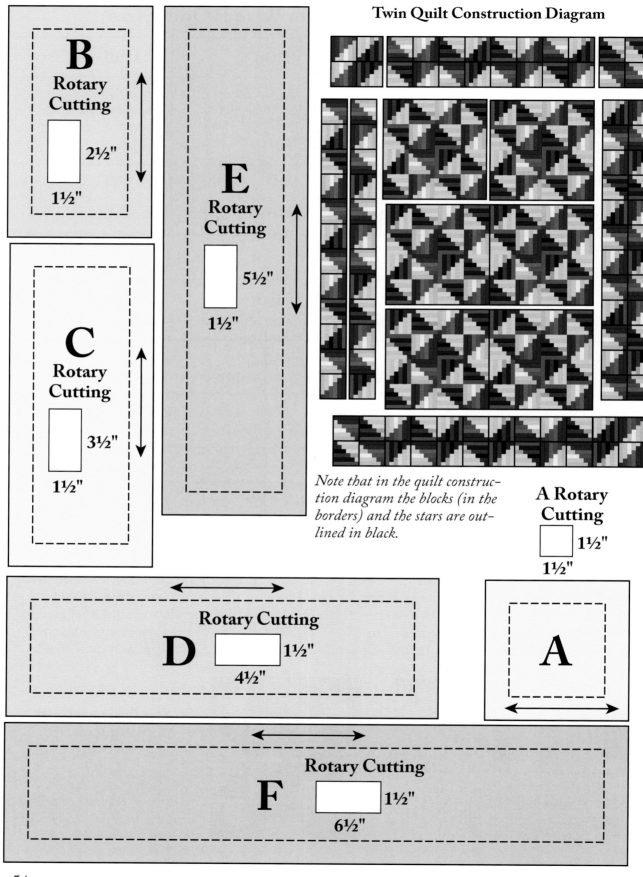

B
Rotary
Cutting

2½"

1½"

C
Rotary
Cutting

3½"

1½"

E
Rotary
Cutting

5½"

1½"

Twin Quilt Construction Diagram

Note that in the quilt construction diagram the blocks (in the borders) and the stars are outlined in black.

A Rotary Cutting

1½"

1½"

Rotary Cutting

D

1½"

4½"

A

Rotary Cutting

F

1½"

6½"

Quilt Construction

Join 16 blocks in 4 rows of 4 blocks each to make stars, turning blocks as shown on page 53. Make one star for the wall quilt, 6 for the twin, and 9 for the queen size.

Join stars in rows as shown in the quilt construction diagram for your quilt size. Press seam allowances to one side. Join rows to complete the quilt center.

To make a border, join blocks in two rows and join rows, turning blocks as shown in the quilt construction diagram. Notice that the orientation of the blocks changes in the corners. Make 4 borders. Attach side borders, then top and bottom borders to complete the quilt top. Press it well.

Wall Quilt Construction Diagram

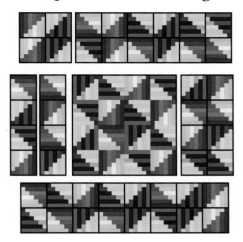

Note that in the quilt construction diagrams the blocks (in the borders) and the stars are outlined in black.

Queen Quilt Construction Diagram

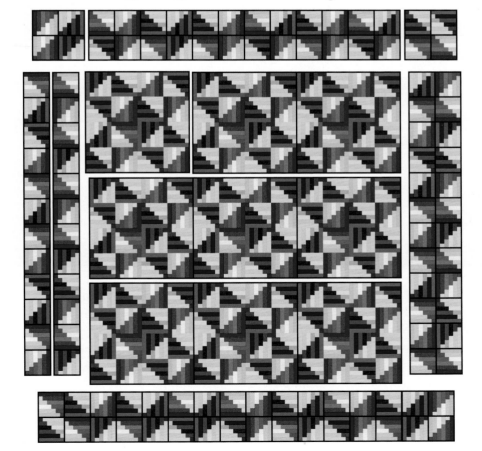

Quilt Finishing

Trim off selvages and square up the backing fabric. Cut out the backing panels as described in the cutting chart. Pin and stitch them.

At this point, you may send out the top for quilting. If you will be hand or machine quilting it yourself, plan the quilting and mark it if necessary. Margy Sieck machine quilted concentric circles all over my Rogue River Log Cabin.

Lay the backing face down, and center the batting and the quilt top, face up, over it. Baste with thread or safety pins, trying to avoid the path of your planned quilting. Quilt and bind to finish.

55

Romeo and Juliet

104" square queen-sized quilt designed and pieced by Judy Martin. Quilted by Linda Mae Diny. Reproductions of mid-nineteenth century prints give this quilt a traditional feeling. This quilt was made with a block-by-block plan. Each block has its own set of three or four fabrics. The background is scrappy. The inner and outer borders are made from fat quarters and leftovers.

When making a block-by-block quilt, I like to plan the fabrics for one or two blocks at a time. This approach is perfect when your quilting time is limited and you are likely to be interrupted. By cutting and sewing two to four blocks at a time, you can stack your fabrics for cutting. You can also chain piece, alternating units for one block, then the other.

Illustrated cutting instructions for the kite-shaped B patch are with the templates on page 58.

Yardage, Dimensions, & Number of Blocks for Various Quilt Sizes

Yardage	Queen	Twin	Wall
Cream Prints	7¾ yds./31 fat qtrs.	6½ yds./26 fat qtrs.	2½ yds./10 fat qtrs.
Navy Prints	4¾ yds./19 fat qtrs.	3¾ yds./15 fat qtrs.	2 yds./8 fat qtrs.
Various Brights	2¾ yds./11 fat qtrs.	2½ yds./10 fat qtrs.	1¼ yds./5 fat qtrs.
Binding	¾ yd.	½ yd.	½ yd.
Backing	10 yds.	7½ yds.	4¼ yds.
Quilt Dimensions	104" x 104"	75" x 104"	60½" x 60½"
Block Sizes	14½" and 8½"	14½" and 8½"	14½" and 8½"
Number of Blocks	13 X, 12 Y, 24 Z	8 X, 7 Y, 20 Z	2 X, 2 Y, 12 Z
Set	5 x 5	3 x 5	2 x 2

 Cutting Requirements for Various Quilt Sizes

Fabric	Queen #18" Strips #borders	Queen #Patches border size	Twin #18" Strips #borders	Twin #Patches border size	Wall #18" Strips #borders	Wall #Patches border size
Cream Prints Borders	2 @	3½" x 79"	2 @	3½" x 73"	2 @	3½" x 35½"
	2 @	3½" x 73"	2 @	3½" x 50"	2 @	3½" x 29½"
⊠ 7¼" x 7¼"	7	52 H	4	32 H	1	8 H
☐ 6½" x 6½"	12	24 J	7	14 J	2	4 J
☐ 4¾" x 4¾"	34	100 I	20	60 I	6	16 I
⊠ 4¾" x 4¾"	12	144 D	9	108 D	5	56 D
☐ 3" x 6½"	12	24 K	10	20 K	6	12 K
☐ 3" x 3"	27	132 L	21	101 L	11	54 L
Navy Prints Borders	2 @	4¾" x 104½"	2 @	4¾" x 96"	2 @	4¾" x 61"
	2 @	4¾" x 96"	2 @	4¾" x 75½"	2 @	4¾" x 52½"
⊠ 4¾" x 4¾"	5	52 D	3	32 D	1	8 D
⊠ 3⅞" x 3⅞"	13	104 G	8	64 G	2	16 G
☐ 1¾" x 3"	11	52 F	7	32 F	2	8 F
☐ 1¾" x 1¾"	6	52 E	4	32 E	1	8 E
◁ 3⅜" x 3⅜"	29	288 B	22	216 B	12	112 B
Various Brights						
☐ 6½" x 6½"	12	24 J	10	20 J	6	12 J
☐ 4" x 4"	13	49 A	9	35 A	4	16 A
◁ 3⅜" x 3⅜"	11	104 B	7	64 B	2	16 B
⊠ 1⅞" x 1⅞"	11	196 C	8	140 C	4	64 C
Binding		2" x 430"		2" x 375"		2" x 260"
Backing	3 panels @	38" x 112"	3 panels @	38" x 83"	2 panels @	35" x 69"

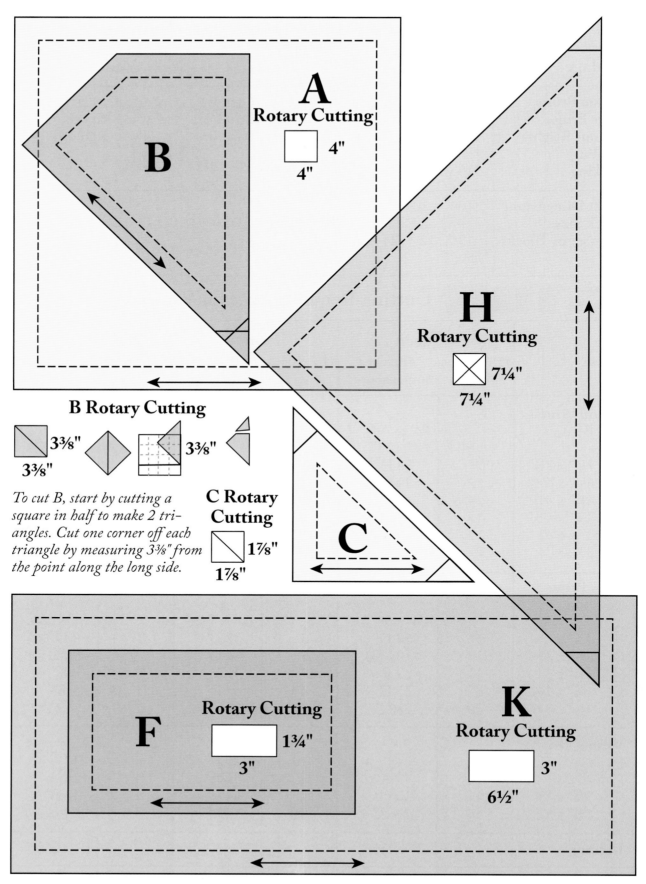

A
Rotary Cutting

4"
4"

B

H
Rotary Cutting

7¼"
7¼"

B Rotary Cutting

3⅜"
3⅜"
3⅜"

To cut B, start by cutting a square in half to make 2 triangles. Cut one corner off each triangle by measuring 3⅜" from the point along the long side.

C Rotary Cutting

1⅞"
1⅞"

C

F
Rotary Cutting

1¾"
3"

K
Rotary Cutting

3"
6½"

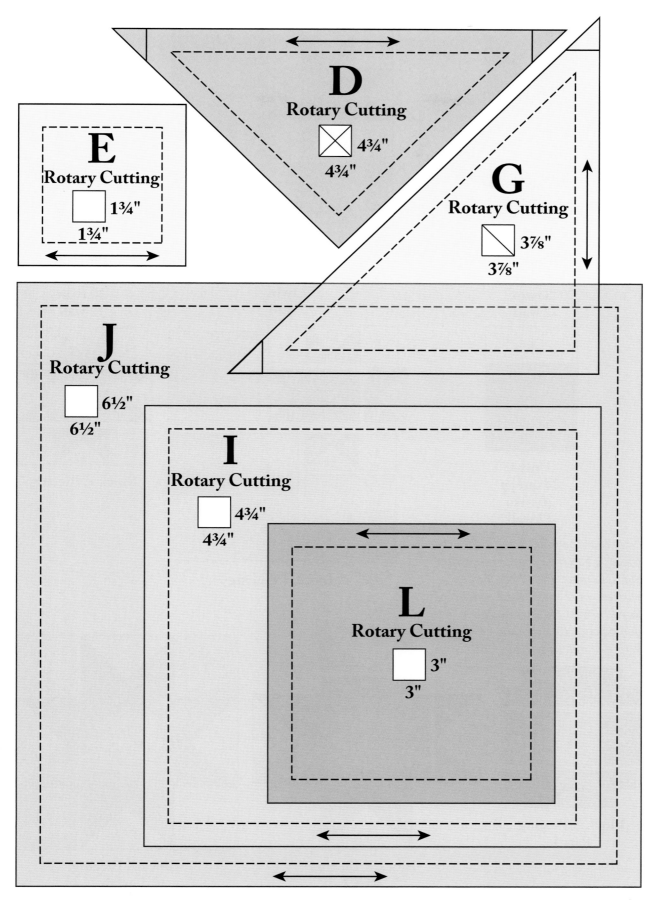

D
Rotary Cutting
⊠ 4¾"
4¾"

E
Rotary Cutting
□ 1¾"
1¾"

G
Rotary Cutting
◲ 3⅞"
3⅞"

J
Rotary Cutting
□ 6½"
6½"

I
Rotary Cutting
□ 4¾"
4¾"

L
Rotary Cutting
□ 3"
3"

59

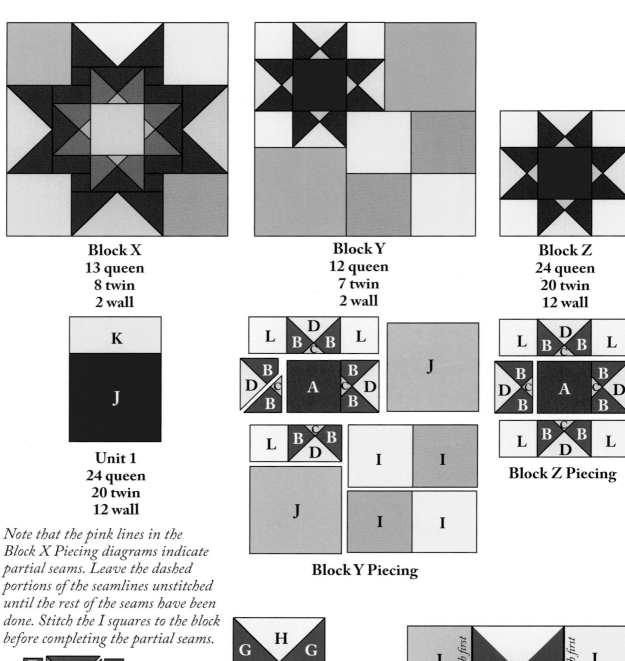

Block X
13 queen
8 twin
2 wall

Block Y
12 queen
7 twin
2 wall

Block Z
24 queen
20 twin
12 wall

Unit 1
24 queen
20 twin
12 wall

Block Z Piecing

Block Y Piecing

Note that the pink lines in the Block X Piecing diagrams indicate partial seams. Leave the dashed portions of the seamlines unstitched until the rest of the seams have been done. Stitch the I squares to the block before completing the partial seams.

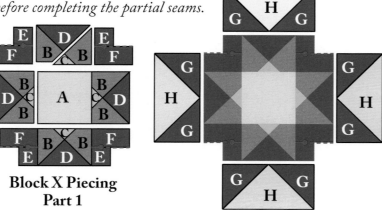

**Block X Piecing
Part 1**

**Block X Piecing
Part 2**

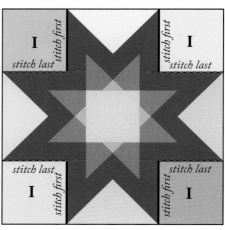

**Block X Piecing
Part 3**

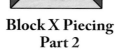

Block and Unit Construction

Note that the navy is for the star points of Y and Z Blocks and the large outer star of the X blocks. Brights are for the square and triangles at each star's center and the points of small stars in X blocks. The bright points of X blocks' inner stars should contrast with navy.

Make Y and Z blocks as shown on page 60. Press seam allowances of stars in a clockwise direction. For the Y blocks, notice that you sew the J's and I's to the star points before you sew the bottom two star points to the star. When you add the J's to the star points, press seams toward J. Press the seam allowances of the I squares to oppose each other.

To make X blocks, refer to the figures at the bottom of page 60.

Part 1. Sewing starts the same as for the Z block, though the colors are different. However, instead of L's you will have E-F segments. Each E is sewn to F with a partial seam. Be sure to arrange all F's as shown. Sew star points, E-F segments, and A's to make rows. Join rows.

Part 2. Sew two G's to each H, pressing toward G's. Sew four of these to the star as shown. Press seams away from block center.

Part 3: Stitch I's to the E-G sides of the star. Finally, complete the four partial seams to join I to F-G sides of the star. Make X blocks in the quantity listed for your quilt size.

Make Unit 1's for borders as shown on page 60. Press seams toward J's.

Queen Quilt Construction

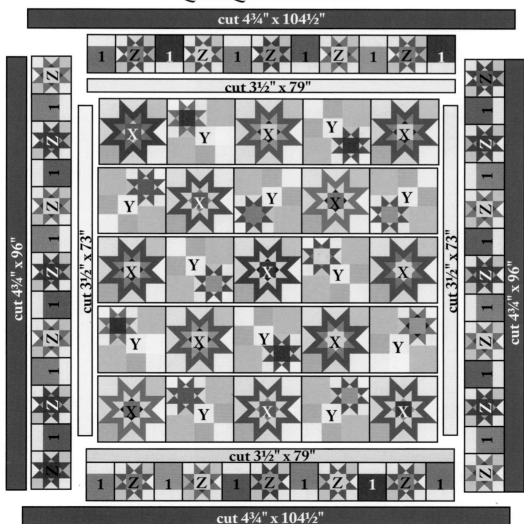

Quilt Construction

Join X and Y blocks alternately to make rows as shown in the quilt diagram for your quilt size. Press seams toward Y's. Join rows.

Add cream borders. Press seam allowances toward the borders.

Make pieced borders by joining Unit 1's and Z blocks in a row, turning every second Unit 1 the opposite direction, as shown. Press seam allowances away from the stars. Sew the pieced borders to the quilt. Press seam allowances toward the cream borders.

Finally, add the navy borders. Press seam allowances toward the navy borders.

Wall Quilt Construction

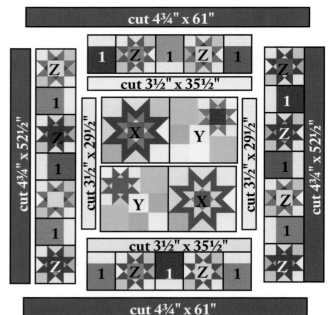

Twin Quilt Construction

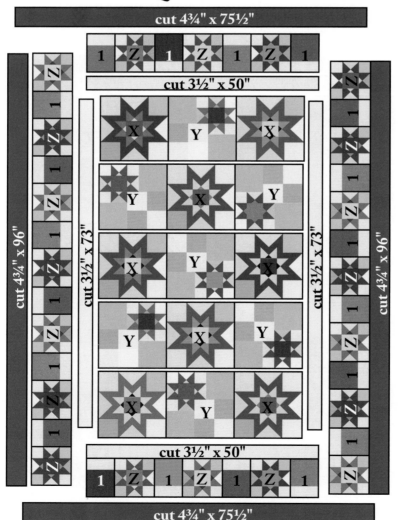

Quilt Finishing

Prewash and press the backing fabric. Trim off selvages and square up the fabric. Cut out backing panels in the size and quantity listed in the cutting chart. Pin and seam together the backing panels.

At this point, you may send out the top to have it quilted. If you will be hand or machine quilting it yourself, plan the quilting and mark it if necessary. Linda Mae Diny outline quilted the stars and quilted curlicues in the background and cables in the border.

Unless your quilting frame has rollers for batting and backing, you will need to baste the layers. On the floor or other large surface, lay the backing face down, and center the batting and the quilt top, face up, over it. Thread baste or pin baste with safety pins, trying to avoid the path of your planned quilting. Quilt, remove any markings, and bind to finish.

62

Hollywood Boulevard

74" x 98" twin quilt designed and pieced by Judy Martin; quilted by Renae Hadda-din. The Japanese-style prints in the border squares and star centers set the style, though many of the prints in other areas are not Japanese at all. I was afraid the stars would not show up if I used busy, multi-colored Japanese scraps for star points. I drew my color scheme from my stash of Japanese prints and repeated these colors in the other prints.

Yardage, Dimensions, & Number of Blocks for Various Quilt Sizes

Yardage	Queen	Twin	Wall
Cream Print	7¼ yds.	5¼ yds.	3⅜ yds.
Tan Print	3 yds.	2 yds.	1 yd.
Bright Prints	4 yds./16 fat qtrs.	3 yds./12 fat qtrs.	1¼ yds./5 fat qtrs.
Binding	¾ yd.	¾ yd.	½ yd.
Backing	9⅜ yds.	7¼ yds.	3½ yds.
Quilt Dimensions	98" x 98"	74" x 98"	50" x 50"
Block Size	10"	10"	10"
Number of Blocks	36 blocks set 6 x 6	24 blocks set 4 x 6	9 blocks set 3 x 3

 ## Cutting Requirements for Various Quilt Sizes

Fabric	Queen #18" Strips # borders	Queen #Patches border size	Twin #18" Strips # borders	Twin #Patches border size	Wall #18" Strips # borders	Wall #Patches border size
Cream Print						
Borders	1 @	2½" x 78½"	1 @	4½" x 72½"	1 @	2½" x 38½"
Borders	1 @	4½" x 76½"	1 @	2½" x 72½"	1 @	2½" x 36½"
Borders	1 @	2½" x 76½"	1 @	4½" x 54½"		
Borders	1 @	4½" x 72½"	1 @	2½" x 54½"		
⊠ 5¼" x 5¼"	12	144 C	8	96 C	3	36 C
☐ 4½" x 4½"					1	1 A
☐ 2½" x 12½"	36*	36 G	24*	24 G	9*	9 G
☐ 2½" x 10½"	36*	36 F	24*	24 F	9*	9 F
☐ 2½" x 6½"	0*	2 H	0*	1 H	0*	1 H
☐ 2½" x 4½"	41*	159 E	33*	123 E	4*	59 E
☐ 2½" x 2½"	35*	275 D	28*	211 D	8*	59 D
Tan Print						
⊠ 5¼" x 5¼"	6	72 C	4	48 C	2	18 C
◩ 2⅞" x 2⅞"	15	144 B	10	96 B	4	36 B
☐ 2½" x 4½"	14	41 E	12	36 E	7	19 E
☐ 2½" x 2½"	29	171 D	24	140 D	6	35 D
Bright Prints						
☐ 4½" x 4½"	42	124 A	34	100 A	11	31 A
◩ 2⅞" x 2⅞"	29	288 B	20	192 B	8	72 B
Binding		2" x 410"		2" x 360"		2" x 215"
Backing	3 panels @	36" x 106"	3 panels @	36" x 82"	2 panels @	29½" x 58"

Cut 1 E along with G. Cut 1 H (as needed) along with F; then cut 2 D's with each remaining F.

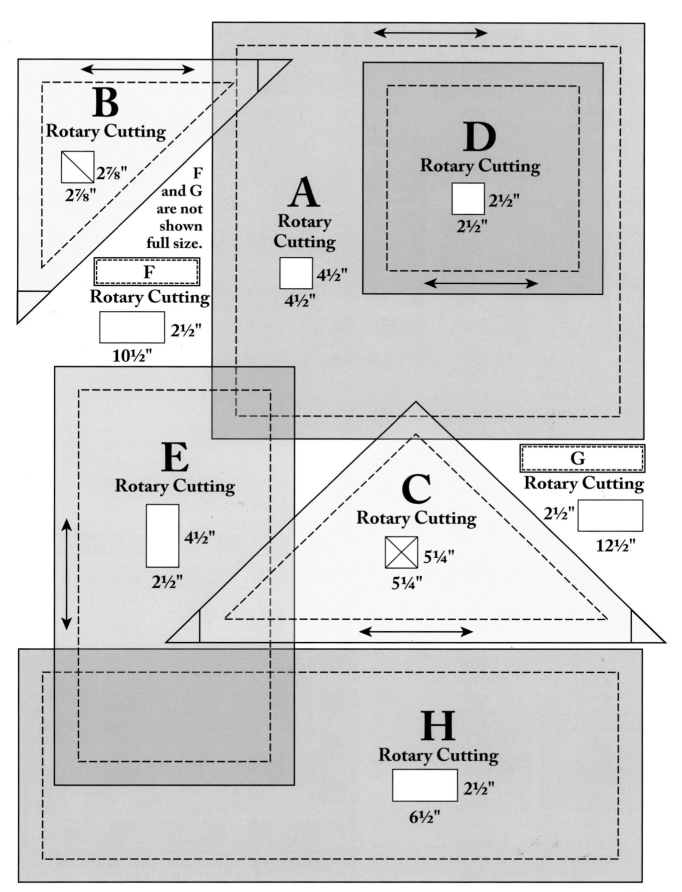

B
Rotary Cutting

2⅞"
2⅞"

F and G are not shown full size.

A
Rotary Cutting

4½"
4½"

D
Rotary Cutting

2½"
2½"

F
Rotary Cutting

2½"
10½"

E
Rotary Cutting

4½"
2½"

C
Rotary Cutting

5¼"
5¼"

G
Rotary Cutting

2½"
12½"

H
Rotary Cutting

2½"
6½"

65

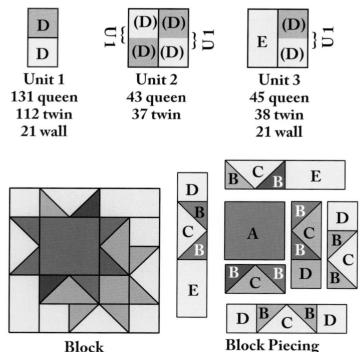

Unit 1
131 queen
112 twin
21 wall

Unit 2
43 queen
37 twin

Unit 3
45 queen
38 twin
21 wall

Block
36 queen
24 twin
9 wall

Block Piecing

Unit Construction

Join cream D's and tan D's to make the listed number of Unit 1's. Press seams toward the tan. These will be used to make Units 2 and 3. For Unit 2, join two Unit 1's, turning them as shown. For Unit 3, sew E to Unit 1 as shown; press seams toward E. Make the listed number of Units 2 and 3.

Block Construction

Join B's and C's as shown at left; press away from C. Stitch one of the tan and bright ones to a bright A. Press seams toward A. To the remaining tan and bright B-C-B, add a tan D as shown; press seams toward D. Add to the star center and press seams toward A.

Add cream D's and E's to the remaining B-C-B's as shown; press seams toward D's and E's. Referring to the block diagram, add the parts in this order: right side, bottom, top, and left. Press the first three of these seams toward the center. Press seams of left side away from center. Make the listed quantity.

Blocks with Strips Added

Add F and G strips to the blocks as shown below. Quantities of each strip placement are listed for three quilt sizes.

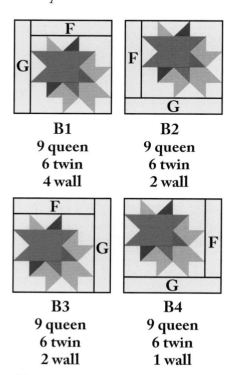

B1
9 queen
6 twin
4 wall

B2
9 queen
6 twin
2 wall

B3
9 queen
6 twin
2 wall

B4
9 queen
6 twin
1 wall

Wall Quilt Construction

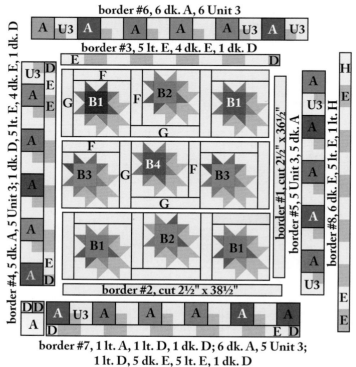

border #6, 6 dk. A, 6 Unit 3

border #3, 5 lt. E, 4 dk. E, 1 dk. D

border #4, 5 dk. A, 5 Unit 3; 1 dk. D, 5 lt. E, 4 dk. E, 1 dk. D

border #1, cut 2½" x 36½"

border #5, 5 Unit 3, 5 dk. A

border #8, 6 dk. E, 5 lt. E, 1 lt. H

border #2, cut 2½" x 38½"

border #7, 1 lt. A, 1 lt. D, 1 dk. D; 6 dk. A, 5 Unit 3; 1 lt. D, 5 dk. E, 5 lt. E, 1 dk. D

Quilt Construction

Sew a cream F and a cream G to each block, referring to the diagram at the bottom left of page 66. Press seams away from the blocks.

Join blocks to form rows. Turn blocks so that each shadow is to the right and bottom of its star. Press seam allowances away from the stars. Join rows, being careful to keep each block turned according to the diagram.

Join remaining cream and tan squares and rectangles to make the narrow pieced borders, pressing seams toward the tan.

Join A's, Unit 2's, and Unit 3's in rows as shown, pressing seams toward A's. Join 2 rows to make each wide border. Attach borders in numerical order, being careful to turn each border to match the quilt diagram.

Queen Quilt Construction

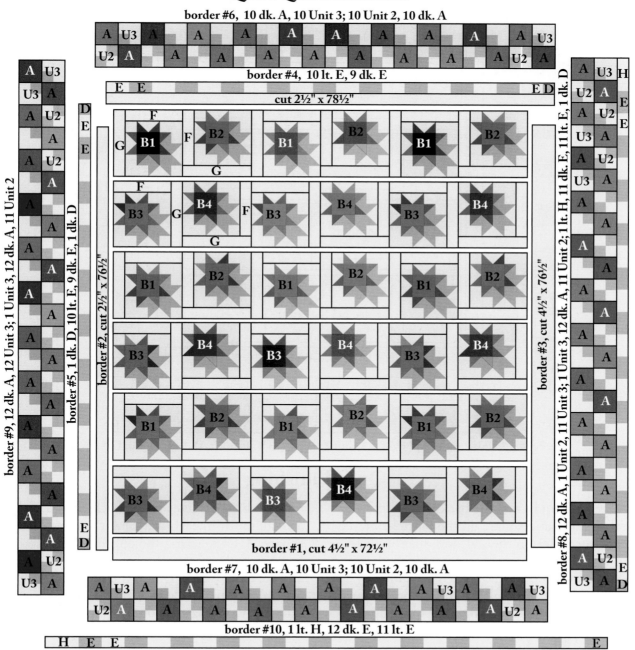

Twin Quilt Construction

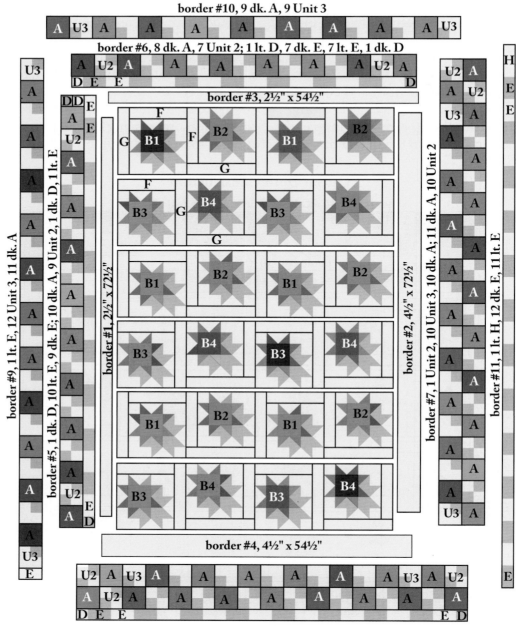

border #10, 9 dk. A, 9 Unit 3

border #6, 8 dk. A, 7 Unit 2; 1 lt. D, 7 dk. E, 7 lt. E, 1 dk. D

border #3, 2½" x 54½"

border #1, 2½" x 72½"

border #2, 4½" x 72½"

border #9, 1 lt. E, 12 Unit 3, 11 dk. A

border #5, 1 dk. D, 10 lt. E, 9 dk. E; 10 dk. A, 9 Unit 2, 1 dk. D, 1 lt. E

border #7, 1 Unit 2, 10 Unit 3, 10 dk. A; 11 dk. A, 10 Unit 2

border #11, 1 lt. H, 12 dk. E, 11 lt. E

border #4, 4½" x 54½"

border #8, 1 Unit 2, 8 dk. A, 7 Unit 3, 1 Unit 2; 9 dk. A, 8 Unit 2; 1 lt. D, 8 dk. E, 8 lt. E, 1 dk. D

Quilt Finishing

Prewash and press the backing fabric. Trim off selvages and square up the fabric. Cut out backing panels in the size and quantity listed in the cutting chart. Pin and seam the backing.

If you will be hand or machine quilting yourself, plan the quilting and mark it if necessary. Renae Haddadin machine quilted my quilt with freehand feathers in the plain borders and extending through the shadows; she quilted diagonal lines in the background and a small motif in each star center and border square. After marking the quilting, baste the layers as follows: Lay the backing face down, and center the batting and the quilt top, face up, over it. Thread baste or pin baste with safety pins, trying to avoid the path of your planned quilting. Quilt, remove any markings, and bind to finish.

Circle of Life

54" x 54" wall quilt designed and pieced by Judy Martin; quilted by Renae Haddadin. People have asked me from time to time whether I ever make quilts that just didn't turn out. The answer is yes. The stars in this block were salvaged from just such a quilt. I had tried putting these stars where the F squares are now in the Monet's Wedding Ring quilt (page 37). They ruined the ring effect I was after, so I decided to remove them. That left me with enough stars to make Circle of Life (and that is also why the two quilts have similar fabrics.)

Scrappy stars in blue, green, rose, purple, and yellow are paired with a nearly solid background fabric. The plain background is ideal for showing off your quilting. Renae did a terrific job of filling the background of my quilt with feathered circles and radiating lines.

The star block is something I designed after happening to see four cut triangles in a stack and turned different directions. I wanted my stars to appear to be made from stacked triangles (though they are simply pieced). I colored the star points with that in mind. You can follow my lead or arrange the colors randomly in your quilt.

Yardage and Dimensions for Various Quilt Sizes

Yardage	Queen	Twin	Wall
Cream Print	7⅝ yds.	5¼ yds.	2¼ yds.
Blue Print	3⅛ yds.	2⅜ yd.	1⅝ yds.
Various Mediums	1½ yds./6 fat qtrs.	1½ yds./6 fat qtrs.	¾ yd./3 fat qtrs.
Binding	¾ yd.	¾ yd.	½ yd.
Backing	9¾ yds.	7⅜ yds.	3¾ yds.
Quilt Dimensions	102" x 102"	75" x 90"	54" x 54"
Block Size	6"	6"	6"
Number of Blocks	48	48	16

Cutting Requirements for Various Quilt Sizes

Fabric	Queen #18" Strips (# borders)	Queen #Patches (border size)	Twin #18" Strips (# borders)	Twin #Patches (border size)	Wall #18" Strips (# borders)	Wall #Patches (border size)
Cream Print Border	4 @	6½" x 78½"	2 @	3½" x 78½"	4 @	6½" x 36½"
	4 @	6½" x 36½"	2 @	3½" x 63½"		
			2 @	6½" x 33½"		
			2 @	5" x 36½"		
			2 @	3½" x 18½"		
☐ 18½" x 18½"	1*	1 G	1*	1 G	1*	1 G
☐ 15½" x 15½"	4	4 M				
☐ 9½" x 9½"	6*	12 F	2*	4 F	2*	4 F
☐ 9½" x 15½"			4	4 L		
☐ 8" x 9½"			2*	4 N		
☐ 6½" x 9½"	2*	4 I	1*	2 I		
☐ 6½" x 6½"	8	16 H	4	8 H		
⊠ 4¼" x 4¼"	12	192 B	12	192 B	4	64 B
☐ 3½" x 9½"			2*	4 K		
☐ 3½" x 6½"	18	36 E	12	24 E	6	12 E
☐ 2" x 6½"			6	12 J		
☐ 2" x 2"	24	192 D	24	192 D	8	64 D
Blue Print Border	4 @	6½" x 103¼"	2 @	3½" x 78½"	4 @	3½" x 55¼"
			2 @	3½" x 63½"		
Various Mediums						
⬦ 5⅜" x 5⅜"	8	48 A	8	48 A	3	16 A
⊠ 4¼" x 4¼"	3	48 B	3	48 B	1	16 B
⬦ 2⅜" x 2⅜"	18	240 C	18	240 C	6	80 C

Cut from strips 19" long.

Cutting Requirements for Various Quilt Sizes, continued

Fabric	Queen		Twin		Wall	
	#18" Strips	#Patches	#18" Strips	#Patches	#18" Strips	#Patches
Binding		2" x 425"		2" x 345"		2" x 230"
Backing	3 panels @	37½" x 110"	3 panels @	33½" x 83"	2 panels @	31¼" x 62"

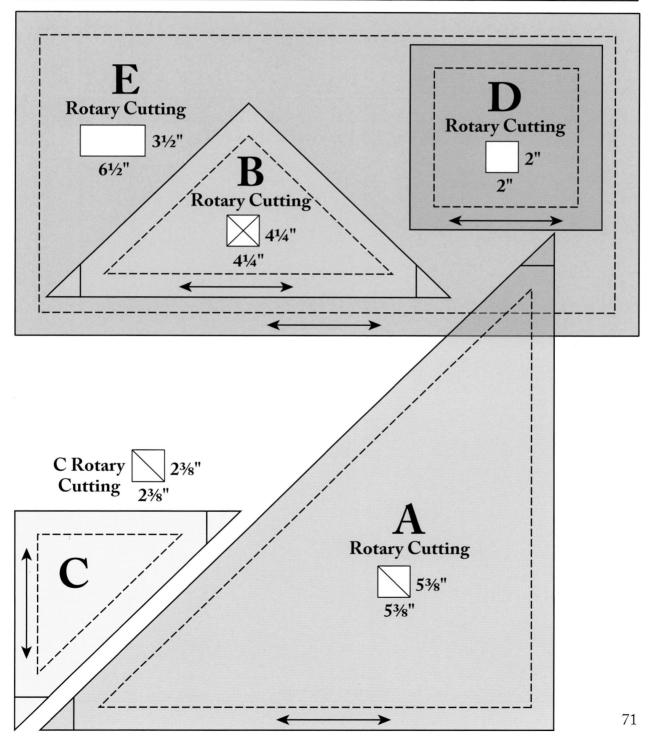

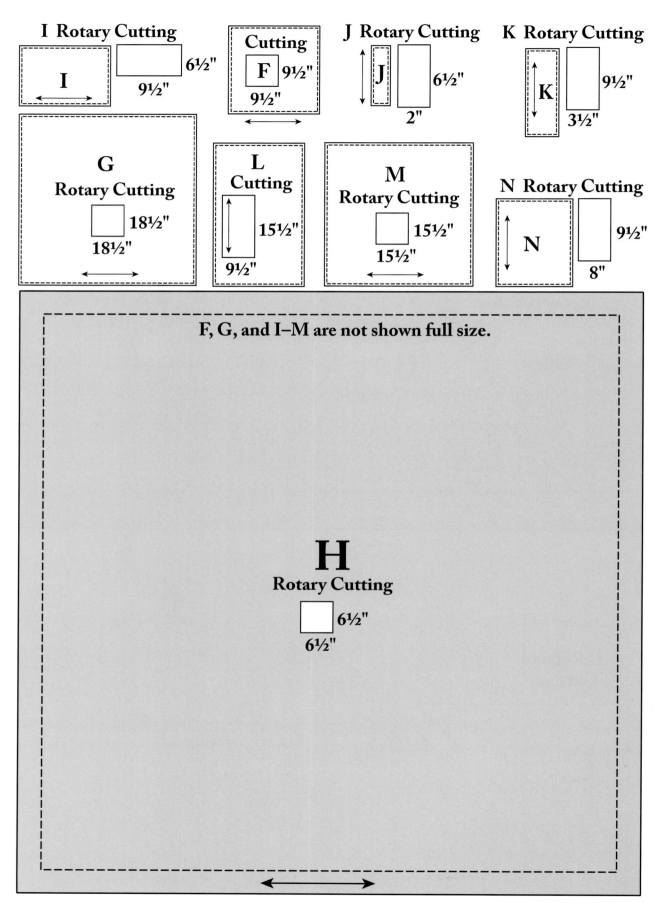

I Rotary Cutting

I

6½"
9½"

Cutting

F 9½"
9½"

J Rotary Cutting

J

6½"
2"

K Rotary Cutting

K

9½"
3½"

G Rotary Cutting

18½"
18½"

L Cutting

15½"
9½"

M Rotary Cutting

15½"
15½"

N Rotary Cutting

N

9½"
8"

F, G, and I–M are not shown full size.

H Rotary Cutting

6½"
6½"

Block Construction

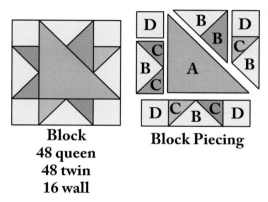

Block
48 queen
48 twin
16 wall

Block Piecing

Arrange patches for a block as shown above, being careful to match the fabric in 2 C-C pairs and 1 C-B pair. Join patches to make the 3 parts shown around A, above. Press seams away from cream B's and toward cream D's. Sew top, then left parts to A before adding bottom part. Press seam allowances at left and bottom toward A; press seam allowance at long side of A away from A. Make the listed number of blocks.

Twin Quilt

Queen Quilt

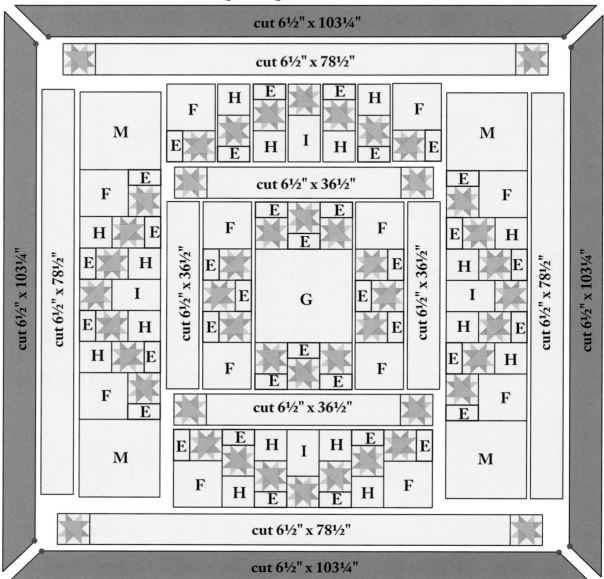

Quilt Construction

Arrange blocks, cream patches E–N, and border strips as shown above or on the next page. Start at the center. Sew an E to each of 12 blocks; press away from the blocks. Join 3 of these in a row, turning them as shown. Make 4 of these sections. Sew one to the top of G and one to the bottom of G. Sew an F to each end of the other 2 sections. Add these to the sides of G. Add 36½"-long borders to 2 sides. Sew a block to each end of the remaining 36½"-long borders. Sew these to the top and bottom to complete the quilt center.

For the queen-size quilt, join blocks and cream patches as shown to make the top and bottom sections. Sew them to the center medallion. Make side sections, and add them. Add cream side borders. Sew a block to each end of the remaining 2 cream borders. Add them to the quilt's top and bottom. Trim off the ends of the blue borders at a 45° angle. Pin and stitch them to all 4 sides of the quilt. Stop ¼" from the raw edges at both ends of each border to allow for the Y seam. Complete the quilt top by stitching borders to one another at

74

the mitered corners, starting at the ends of the seams that attach the borders and ending at the borders' corners.

For the twin-size quilt, join blocks and cream patches as shown to make top and bottom sections. Sew to the center medallion. Make side sections and add them. Join blue and cream border strips in same-size pairs. Sew two of these to the quilt's sides. Add a block to each end of the remaining two, and sew them to the quilt's top and bottom.

For the wall quilt, trim off the ends of the blue borders at a 45° angle. Pin and stitch the borders to all 4 sides of the quilt, stopping ¼" from the ends. Complete the quilt top by pinning and stitching borders to one another at the mitered corners, stitching from precisely the ends of the seams that attached the borders to the outer corners of the quilt.

Twin Quilt Construction

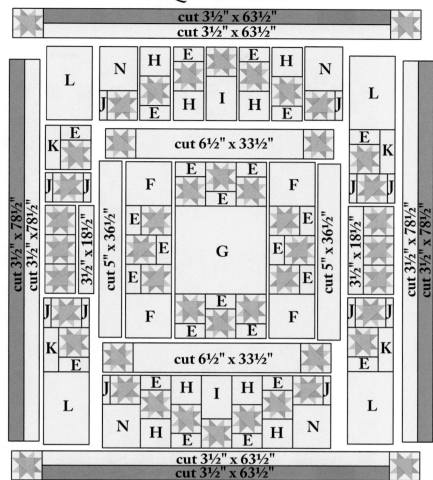

Wall Quilt Construction

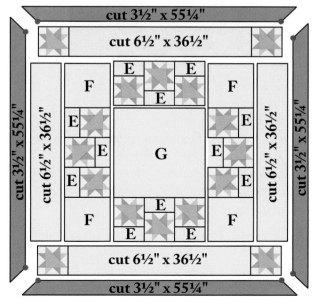

Quilt Finishing

Prewash and press the backing fabric. Trim off selvages and square up the fabric. Cut out backing panels in the size and quantity listed in the cutting chart. Pin and seam together the backing panels.

At this point, you may send out the top for quilting. If you will be hand or machine quilting it yourself, plan the quilting and mark it if necessary. Renae Haddadin machine quilted my Circle of Life with an intricate pattern of feathers, circles, and radiating lines.

Baste the layers together as follows: Lay the backing face down, and center the batting and the quilt top, face up, over it. Thread baste or pin baste with safety pins, trying to avoid the path of your planned quilting. Quilt, remove any markings, and bind to finish.

Celebration

48" x 57" baby quilt designed and pieced by Judy Martin; quilted by Margy Sieck. Bright, whimsical prints are paired with crisp black and white for a youthful look in this quick and easy quilt. A single black print, two or three white prints, and a large variety of hot pink, purple, bright blue, turquoise, lime green, yellow, yellow-orange, and orange prints were used. The bright prints include stylized florals, novelty prints with assorted wildly colored critters, and jaunty geometrics. The black-and-white checked print binding echoes the small squares in the blocks. Asymmetrical borders add to the whimsy.

Yardage and Dimensions for Various Quilt Sizes

Yardage	Queen	Twin	Baby
Black Print **White Prints** **Bright Prints** **Binding** **Backing**	2½ yds. 2½ yds./10 fat qtrs. 7¾ yds./31 fat qtrs. ¾ yd. 9 yds.	2 yds. 2 yds./8 fat qtrs. 6¼ yds./25 fat qtrs. ¾ yd. 7½ yds.	1 yd. 1 yd./4 fat qtrs. 2½ yds./10 fat qtrs. ½ yd. 3½ yds.
Quilt Dimensions **Block Size** **Number of Blocks** **Set**	93" x 93" 9" 41 Y, 40 Z blocks 9 x 9	75" x 93" 9" 32 Y, 31 Z blocks 7 x 9	48" x 57" 9" 10 Y, 10 Z blocks 4 x 5

 Cutting Requirements for Various Quilt Sizes

Fabric	Queen #18" Strips	Queen #Patches	Twin #18" Strips	Twin #Patches	Baby #18" Strips	Baby #Patches
Black Print ☐ 2" x 2"	90	718 A	74	586 A	31	244 A
White Prints ☐ 2" x 2"	90	718 A	74	586 A	31	244 A
Bright Prints ☐ 3½" x 3½"	151	602 B	121	482 B	46	182 B
Binding		2" x 390"		2" x 350"		2" x 225"
Backing	3 panels @	34½" x 101"	3 panels @	34" x 83"	2 panels @	33" x 56"

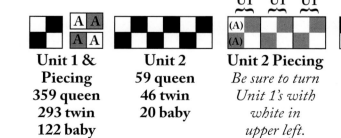
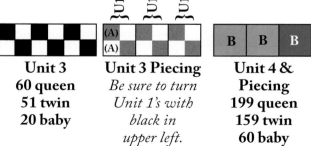

Unit 1 & Piecing	Unit 2	Unit 2 Piecing	Unit 3	Unit 3 Piecing	Unit 4 & Piecing
359 queen 293 twin 122 baby	59 queen 46 twin 20 baby	*Be sure to turn Unit 1's with white in upper left.*	60 queen 51 twin 20 baby	*Be sure to turn Unit 1's with black in upper left.*	199 queen 159 twin 60 baby

Make the listed number of Unit 1's. Reserve 2 of them for the border ends. Use the rest to make

Unit 2 and Unit 3 in the quantities listed. Units 2, 3, and 4 are used to make blocks and borders.

Unit Construction

Join each black A square to a white A square; press seam allowances toward the black. Join these to make four-patch Unit 1's in the quantity listed for your quilt size. Join 3 Unit 1's to make each Unit 2. Press seam allowances to one side. Turn Unit 1's as shown and similarly make Unit 3's. Join 3 B's to make each Unit 4. Press seams to one side.

Block Construction

Reserve 18 (queen), 14 (twin), or 10 (baby) Unit 2's; 20 (queen), 20 (twin), or 10 (baby) Unit 3's; and 37 (queen), 33 (twin), or 20 (baby) Unit 4's for the borders. Join 2 Unit 4's and 1 Unit 2 to make a Y block. Make the quantity listed below. Join 2 Unit 4's and 1 Unit 3 to make a Z block. Make the quantity listed for your quilt size. Press seam allowances toward the B end.

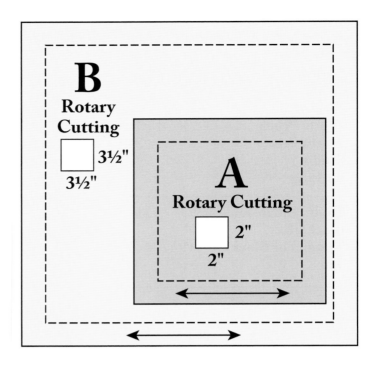

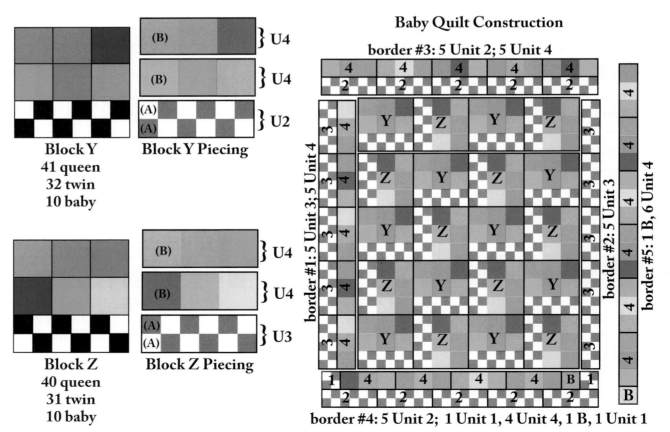

Block Y
41 queen
32 twin
10 baby

Block Y Piecing

Block Z
40 queen
31 twin
10 baby

Block Z Piecing

Baby Quilt Construction

border #3: 5 Unit 2; 5 Unit 4

border #1: 5 Unit 3; 5 Unit 4

border #2: 5 Unit 3

border #5: 1 B, 6 Unit 4

border #4: 5 Unit 2; 1 Unit 1, 4 Unit 4, 1 B, 1 Unit 1

78

Queen Quilt Construction
border #1: 9 Unit 2; 9 Unit 4

border #2: 9 Unit 2; 9 Unit 4

border #3: 10 Unit 3, 1 B; 1 Unit 1, 1 B; 9 Unit 4, 1 Unit 1, 1B

border #4: 10 Unit 3, 1 B; 10 Unit 4, 1B

Quilt Construction

Refer to the quilt diagram for your chosen size on this page, the previous page, or the following page. Join blocks to make rows, turning Y blocks so their black and white checks are at the bottom and turning Z blocks so their checks are at the left. Join rows.

Join remaining like units end to end to make border rows as shown in the quilt construction diagrams. Also add B patches and Unit 1's to the ends as shown. Note the way the borders are turned in the diagrams.

For the queen and twin sizes, join the Unit 4 rows to the checkered rows. Pin and stitch top and bottom borders, then side borders, to the quilt center.

For the baby quilt, join the Unit 4 rows to the checkered rows of the left, top, and bottom. Pin and stitch the Unit 3-Unit 4 border to the left of the quilt and the Unit 3 border to right of quilt. Pin and stitch Unit 2-Unit 4 borders to the top and bottom of the quilt. Finally, sew the Unit 4 border to the right.

Twin Quilt Construction

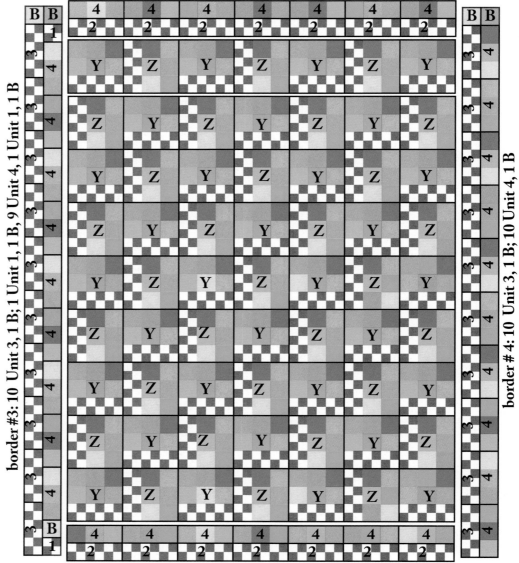

border #1: 7 Unit 2, 7 Unit 4

border #2: 7 Unit 2, 7 Unit 4

border #3: 10 Unit 3, 1 B; 1 Unit 1, 1 B, 9 Unit 4, 1 Unit 1, 1 B

border # 4: 10 Unit 3, 1 B; 10 Unit 4, 1 B

Quilt Finishing

Prewash and press the backing fabric. Trim off selvages and square up the fabric. Cut out backing panels in the size and quantity listed in the cutting chart. Pin and seam together the backing panels.

At this point, you may send out the top for quilting. If you plan to hand or machine quilt it yourself, plan the quilting and mark it if necessary. I would suggest quilting a curvy all-over pattern such as Baptist Fans, clamshells, or something similar.

Unless your quilting frame has rollers for batting and backing, you will need to baste the layers. To baste, lay the backing face down and center the batting and the quilt top, face up, over it. Thread baste or pin baste with safety pins, trying to avoid the path of your planned quilting. Quilt and bind to finish.

Cooperstown Stars

72" x 96" twin-sized quilt designed and pieced by Judy Martin; quilted by Nichole Webb. A warm palette of country-style prints sets the style for this quilt. Blocks, background, and borders are all scrappy. A color scheme of tan, grape, pumpkin, green, *black, brown, and gold provided a starting point. Fabrics were sorted and used in specific places. Light tans form the background; dark tans the inner border. Darks were used for stars and border; mediums for the small stars within the large ones.*

Yardage and Dimensions for Various Quilt Sizes

Yardage	Queen	Twin	Wall
Light Tan Prints	5½ yds./22 fat qtrs.	3¾ yds./15 fat qtrs.	1¾ yds./7 fat qtrs.
Dark Tan Prints	2¾ yds./11 fat qtrs.	2¼ yds./9 fat qtrs.	1½ yds./6 fat qtrs.
Various Darks	5½ yds./22 fat qtrs.	4¼ yds./17 fat qtrs.	2 yds./8 fat qtrs.
Small Stars in Z	1 yds./4 fat qtrs.	1 yd./4 fat qtrs.	½ yd./2 fat qtrs.
Binding	¾ yd.	¾ yd.	½ yd.
Backing	9⅛ yds.	6⅛ yds.	4 yds.
Quilt Dimensions	96" x 96"	72" x 96"	60" x 60"
Block Size	6" and 12"	6" and 12"	6" and 12"
Number of Blocks	24 Y, 24 Z	16 Y, 16 Z	8 Y, 5 Z

 **Cutting Requirements for Various Quilt Sizes**

Fabric	Queen #18" Strips	Queen #Patches	Twin #18" Strips	Twin #Patches	Wall #18" Strips	Wall #Patches
Lt. Tan Prints						
☒ 7¼" x 7¼"	13	100 E	9	68 E	3	24 E
☐ 6½" x 6½"	11	22 H	7	14 H	3	6 H
☐ 4¾" x 4¾"	1	2 I	1	2 I	1	2 I
☒ 4¼" x 4¼"	6	96 B	4	64 B	2	32 B
◩ 3⅞" x 3⅞"	11	82 F	9	66 F	5	34 F
☐ 3½" x 3½"	25	98 G	17	66 G	6	22 G
☐ 2" x 2"	12	96 D	8	64 D	4	32 D
Dark Tan Prints						
☒ 7¼" x 7¼"	1	6 E	1	6 E	1	6 E
☐ 6½" x 6½"	24	46 H	19	38 H	11	22 H
☒ 4¼" x 4¼"	1	8 B	1	8 B	1	8 B
◩ 3⅞" x 3⅞"	1	6 F	1	6 F	1	6 F
☐ 3½" x 3½"	2	8 G	2	8 G	2	8 G
☐ 2" x 2"	1	8 D	1	8 D	1	8 D
Various Darks						
◩ 5⅜" x 5⅜"	5	26 A	3	18 A	2	10 A
☒ 4¼" x 4¼"	9	138 B	7	98 B	3	46 B
◩ 3⅞" x 3⅞"	38	304 F	28	224 F	13	104 F
☐ 3½" x 3½"	31	124 G	27	108 G	19	76 G
◩ 2⅜" x 2⅜"	10	130 C	7	90 C	4	50 C
☐ 2" x 2"	14	112 D	10	80 D	5	36 D

Cutting Requirements for Various Quilt Sizes, continued

Fabric	Queen		Twin		Wall	
	#18" Strips	#Patches	#18" Strips	#Patches	#18" Strips	#Patches
Sm. Stars in Z ◇ 5⅜" x 5⅜" ⊠ 4¼" x 4¼" ◇ 2⅜" x 2⅜"	5 2 10	28 A 28 B 140 C	4 2 8	20 A 20 B 100 C	2 1 4	9 A 9 B 45 C
Binding		2" x 400"		2" x 350"		2" x 255"
Backing	3 panels @	35¼" x 104"	2 panels @	40" x 104"	2 panels @	34½" x 68"

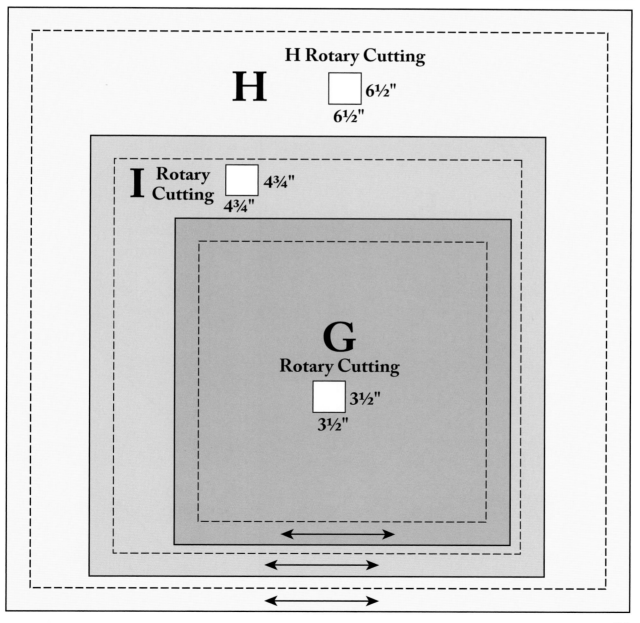

H Rotary Cutting

H 6½"
6½"

I Rotary Cutting 4¾"
4¾"

G
Rotary Cutting 3½"
3½"

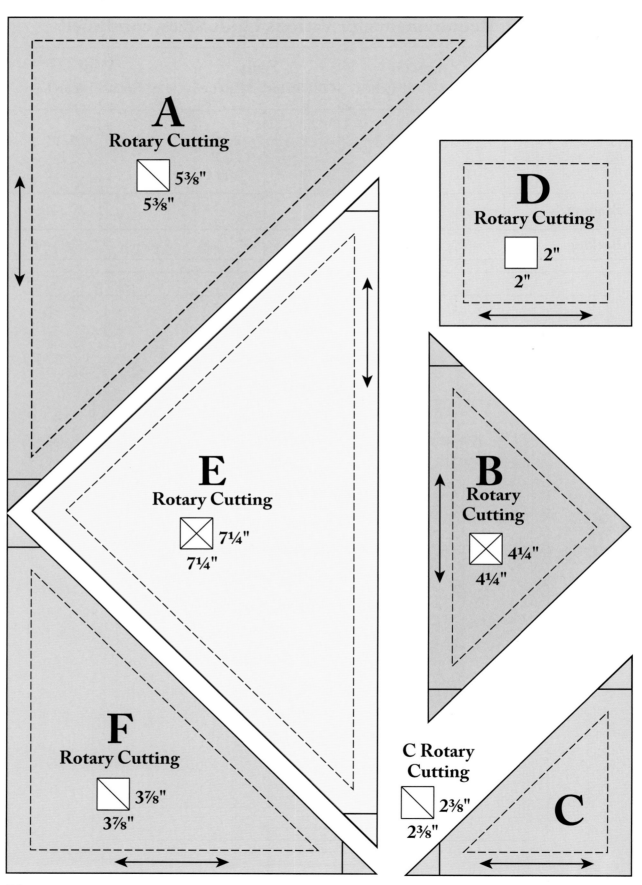

A
Rotary Cutting

5⅜"
5⅜"

D
Rotary Cutting

2"
2"

E
Rotary Cutting

7¼"
7¼"

B
Rotary Cutting

4¼"
4¼"

F
Rotary Cutting

3⅞"
3⅞"

C Rotary Cutting

2⅜"
2⅜"

C

Block and Border Unit Construction

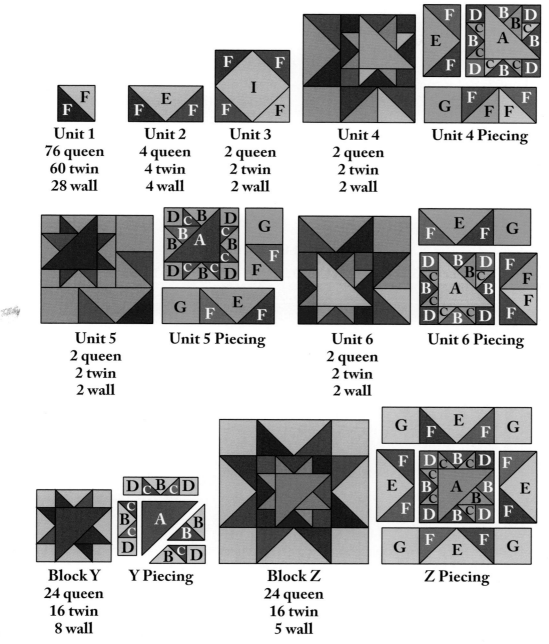

Unit 1
76 queen
60 twin
28 wall

Unit 2
4 queen
4 twin
4 wall

Unit 3
2 queen
2 twin
2 wall

Unit 4
2 queen
2 twin
2 wall

Unit 4 Piecing

Unit 5
2 queen
2 twin
2 wall

Unit 5 Piecing

Unit 6
2 queen
2 twin
2 wall

Unit 6 Piecing

Block Y
24 queen
16 twin
8 wall

Y Piecing

Block Z
24 queen
16 twin
5 wall

Z Piecing

The cutting and sewing of this quilt is no more difficult than a basic star, but the borders (which give the quilt its pizzazz) require a variety of units to keep straight.

The dark scraps are used for the large stars, the border triangles, and the small stars in Unit 5 and Block Y. The scraps used for the small stars within larger stars (in Units 4 and 6 and Block Z) are light enough to contrast with the darks. All stars, large and small, should contrast with their backgrounds.

Notice that I matched fabric in pairs of star points; you may follow my diagrams or color star points randomly.

Make blocks and border units in the quantities listed for your quilt size. Refer to the Y piecing diagram for piecing of all small stars. Press seam allowances of Units 1–3 toward the darks. Within each star, press seam allowances away from background triangle and toward background squares. Press away from the small center star of each double star.

Quilt Construction

Refer to the quilt construction diagram for your chosen quilt size. Lay out the blocks on the floor or a design wall, turning blocks as desired. Sew each Y block to a light tan H square or a Unit 3. Refer to the quilt diagram for placement of Unit 3's.

For the queen and twin sizes, alternate these Y sections with Z blocks, and join them to make vertical rows, being careful to place the Unit 3's in the upper left and lower right corners of the quilt center. Note that each row has a Z block on one end and a Y block on the other. Join rows.

For the wall quilt, sew two Y sections to opposite sides of a Z block. Make sure to sew the Unit 3's as shown for placement in the upper left and lower right corners. Sew one of the resulting sections to the remaining Z block with a partial seam, as indicated by the pink in the diagram. Stitch from the ends of the Y and Z blocks to the pink dot, approximately at the other end of the Y block. You will complete this seam later. Add another section to the left side; proceed to the bottom; then the right. After adding the right section, complete the partial seam.

Queen Quilt Construction
border #5, 30 G; 12 H; 8 Unit 1, 1 Unit 2, 11 Unit 1; 1 Unit 6

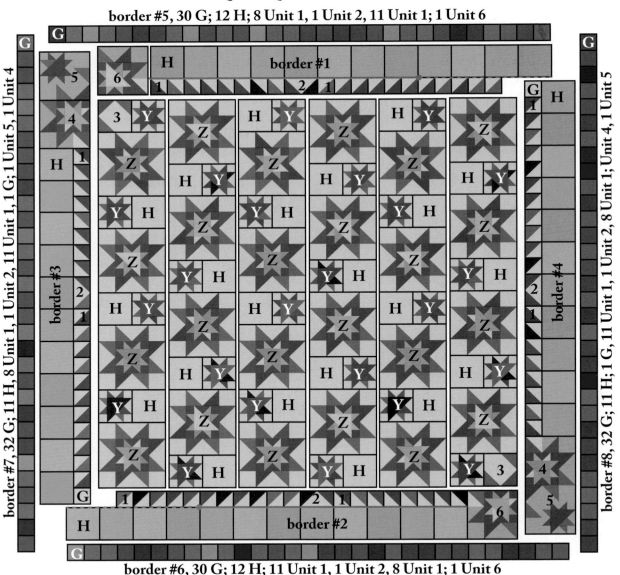

border #6, 30 G; 12 H; 11 Unit 1, 1 Unit 2, 8 Unit 1; 1 Unit 6

Twin Quilt Construction

border #5, 22 G; 8 H; 4 Unit 1, 1 Unit 2, 7 Unit 1; 1 Unit 6

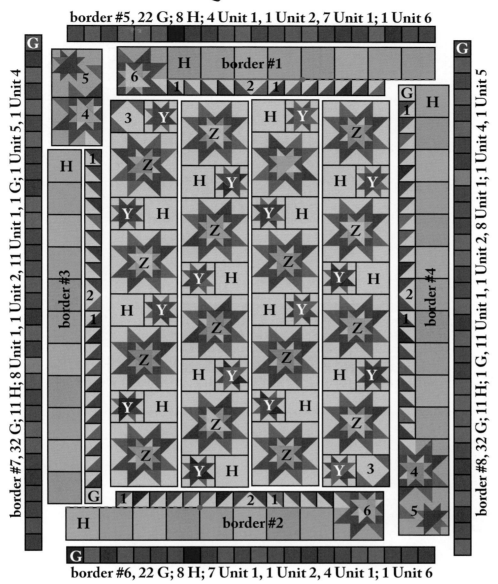

border #6, 22 G; 8 H; 7 Unit 1, 1 Unit 2, 4 Unit 1; 1 Unit 6

For all sizes, join G's in the quantities listed on the quilt diagram to make border strips. Similarly join H's. Join Unit 1's, turning them as indicated, and inserting a Unit 2 where strips of Unit 1's change direction at the center of each side of the quilt. Add a light tan G square to top right and bottom left borders.

For the top and bottom of the quilt, stitch an H border to a Unit 1 border as shown, with a partial seam at one end. That is, stitch where the solid pink line is in the diagram; stop at the pink dot; and leave the pink dashed part free until later. Add a Unit 6 to the left end of the top border and the right end of the bottom. Sew these borders to the quilt.

Join the Unit 1 border to the H border for the two sides of the quilt. Add Units 4 and 5 to one end of each side border as shown. Stitch borders to the sides of the quilt. Complete the partial seams. Add G borders to top and bottom, then sides of the quilt. Press well.

Seam the backing panels; press. Layer the quilt top, batting and backing. Baste the layers together. Quilt as you like. I would suggest outline quilting or in-the-ditch quilting for the stars and border triangles and quilting down the background to make the stars shine. Nichole Webb quilted freehand feathers in the dark and light tan areas, continuing into the dark border. Bind to finish.

Wall Quilt Construction

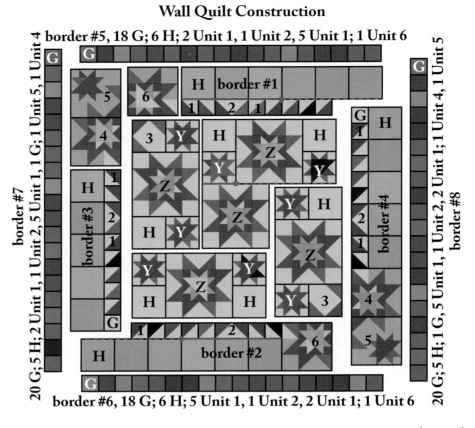

border #5, 18 G; 6 H; 2 Unit 1, 1 Unit 2, 5 Unit 1; 1 Unit 6

border #4

border #7

20 G; 5 H; 2 Unit 1, 1 Unit 2, 5 Unit 1, 1 G; 1 Unit 5, 1 Unit 4

20 G; 5 H; 1 G, 5 Unit 1, 1 Unit 2, 2 Unit 1; 1 Unit 4, 1 Unit 5

border #8

border #6, 18 G; 6 H; 5 Unit 1, 1 Unit 2, 2 Unit 1; 1 Unit 6

Another Look for Cooperstown Stars

54" square wall (or crib) quilt designed by Judy Martin; pieced and quilted by Linda Med-hus. Perky florals and plaids in bright colors completely change the look of Cooperstown Stars. Note also how Linda's light outer border high-lights the center, whereas the darker borders of my quilt emphasize the perimeter. Linda impro-vised with a single fabric for the wide border and chose to leave off the dark outer border entirely.

88

Newport Beach

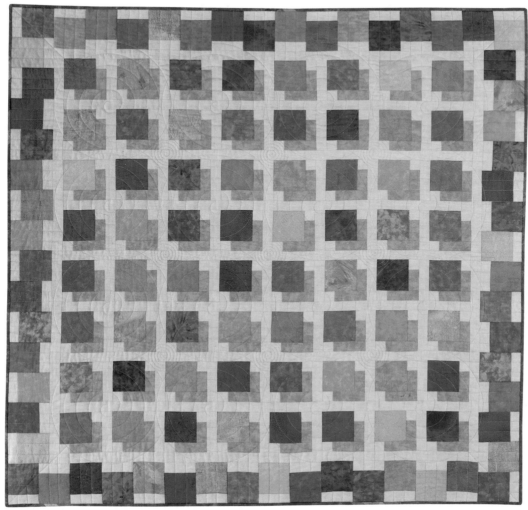

49" x 49" wall or baby quilt designed and pieced by Judy Martin; quilted by Margy Sieck. Contemporary prints that are nearly solid form squares that appear to float over the creamy background. I used colors all around the color wheel, but I limited my scraps to the very brightest and clearest I could find.

I envisioned brightly colored sails when I named this quilt.

I recommend choosing a single background fabric and one shadow fabric for the best shadow effect. The shadow fabric should be darker than the background fabric. I found that the best effect required a bigger difference between background and shadow than I would have thought. With this photograph as a guide, you should be able to choose shadow and background fabrics easily.

Yardage and Dimensions for Various Quilt Sizes

Yardage	Queen	Twin	Baby
Lt. Cream Print	6¼ yds.	4 yds.	2¼ yds.
Tan Print	2¼ yds.	1¾ yds.	¾ yd.
Various Brights	4¾ yds./19 fat qtrs.	3¾ yds./15 fat qtrs.	1¾ yds./7 fat qtrs.
Binding	¾ yd.	¾ yd.	½ yd.
Backing	9⅛ yds.	5⅞ yds.	3⅜ yds.
Quilt Dimensions	95" x 95"	69" x 89"	49" x 49"
Block Size	4" and 3" x 4"	4" and 3" x 4"	4" and 3" x 4"
Number of Blocks	256 blks. set 16 x16	192 blks. set 12 x 16	64 blks. set 8 by 8

Cutting Requirements for Various Quilt Sizes

Fabric	Queen #18" Strips # Borders	Queen #Patches Border Size	Twin #18" Strips # Borders	Twin #Patches Border Size	Baby #18" Strips # Borders	Baby #Patches Border Size
Lt. Cream Print						
Borders	2 @	4½" x 87½"	2 @	1½" x 81½"	2 @	1½" x 41½"
Borders	2 @	4½" x 79½"				
Long Sash	15 @	1½" x 79½"	17 @	1½" x 59½"	9 @	1½" x 39½"
1½" x 4½"	82	244 D	59	176 D	19	56 D
1½" x 3½"	30	120 C	25	100 C	15	60 C
1½" x 1½"	47	512 A	35	384 A	12	128 A
Tan Print						
1½" x 3½"	64	256 C	48	192 C	16	64 C
1½" x 2½"	43	256 B	32	192 B	11	64 B
Various Brights						
3½" x 3½"	94	376 E	73	292 E	31	124 E
Binding		2" x 400"		2" x 335"		2" x 210"
Backing	3 panels @	35" x 103"	2 panels @	39" x 97"	2 panels @	29" x 57"

Block and Unit Construction

Sew a light cream A square to each B and C rectangle cut from your shadow fabric. Press seams toward the shadow. Refer to the block diagrams at right. Sew A-B to each bright E as shown; press seams away from E. Add A-C; press seams away from E. Make the number of blocks required for your quilt size. For border and corner units, sew a light cream C to each remaining bright E; press away from E. For the queen size only, add a light cream D to 4 of the border units to make corner units; press seam allowances away from E.

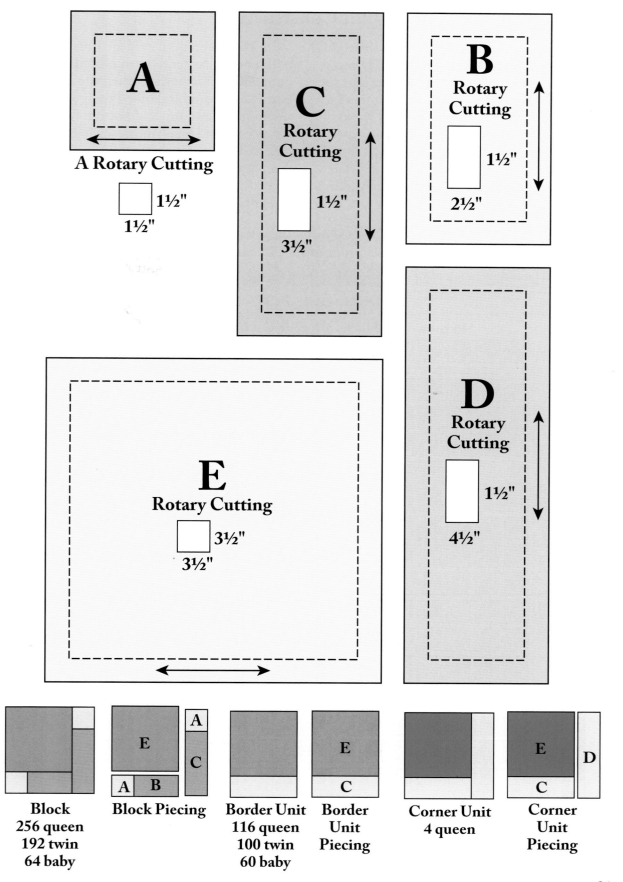

A

A Rotary Cutting

1½"
1½"

C

Rotary Cutting

1½"
3½"

B

Rotary Cutting

1½"
2½"

D

Rotary Cutting

1½"
4½"

E

Rotary Cutting

3½"
3½"

Block
256 queen
192 twin
64 baby

Block Piecing

A
C

E

A B

Border Unit
116 queen
100 twin
60 baby

Border Unit Piecing

E

C

Corner Unit
4 queen

Corner Unit Piecing

E

C

D

Quilt Construction

Lay out blocks with all shadows to the right and bottom of the E squares. Stitch a D rectangle to the right side of each block except the one on the right end of each row. Join these to make a row. Add the last block. Press seams toward the D's. Make all rows. Pin and stitch long sashes between rows.

Join border units as shown in the quilt diagram, turning them to stagger the E's. Make 4 of these pieced borders.

For the queen quilt, add a corner unit to both ends of top and bottom borders. Attach light cream side borders, then top and bottom borders to the quilt. Follow these with pieced side borders and top and bottom borders.

For twin and baby quilts, sew borders the size of long sashes to the quilt's top and bottom. Sew longer light cream borders to sides.

For the twin size, add pieced side borders, then pieced top and bottom borders.

Queen Quilt Construction
border #7, 29 border units + 2 corner units

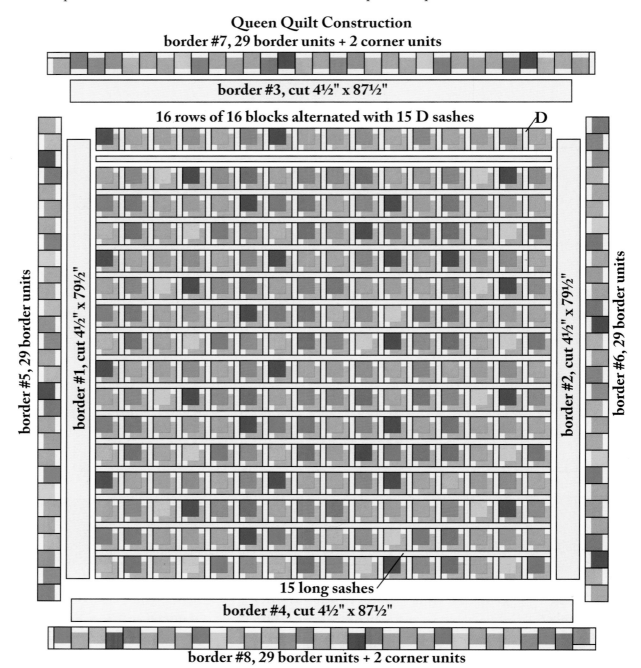

border #3, cut 4½" x 87½"

16 rows of 16 blocks alternated with 15 D sashes   D

border #5, 29 border units

border #1, cut 4½" x 79½"

border #2, cut 4½" x 79½"

border #6, 29 border units

15 long sashes

border #4, cut 4½" x 87½"

border #8, 29 border units + 2 corner units

92

For the baby quilt, attach a pieced border to the bottom of the quilt with a short partial seam as indicated in pink. Add right, top, then left borders. Complete the partial seam.

Quilt Finishing

Prewash and press the backing fabric. Trim off selvages and square up the fabric. Cut out backing panels in the size and quantity listed in the cutting chart. Pin and seam together the backing panels.

At this point, you may send out the top for quilting. If you will be hand or machine quilting it yourself, plan the quilting and mark it if necessary. Margy Sieck machine quilted my

Newport Beach with spirals over the body of the quilt and parallel lines in the borders.

After you mark any quilting, baste the layers together as follows: Lay the backing face down, and center the batting and the quilt top, face up, over it. Thread baste or pin baste with safety pins, trying to avoid the path of your planned quilting. Quilt, remove any markings, and bind to finish.

Twin Quilt Construction
border #7, 23 border units

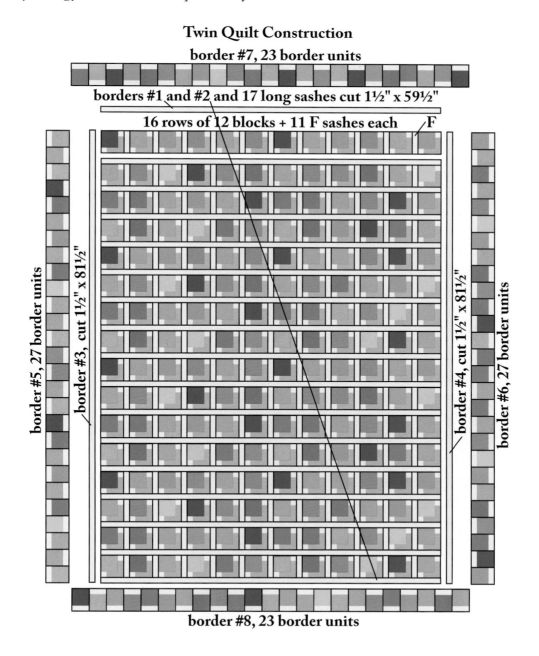

borders #1 and #2 and 17 long sashes cut 1½" x 59½"

16 rows of 12 blocks + 11 F sashes each   F

border #5, 27 border units

border #3, cut 1½" x 81½"

border #4, cut 1½" x 81½"

border #6, 27 border units

border #8, 23 border units

The various quilt sizes all required different treatment in the corners of the pieced borders. For the baby quilt, start with the bottom border. Attach it with a partial seam. I like to stitch just a short distance in this situation so I can attach most of the bottom border after the left border has been added. This allows me to pin both ends and distribute the border evenly when I pin it.

Attach the right border next, aligning its ends with the edge of the bottom pieced border and the long sash at the top.

Similarly attach the top pieced border and the left pieced border.

After attaching the left border, you may complete the partial seam.

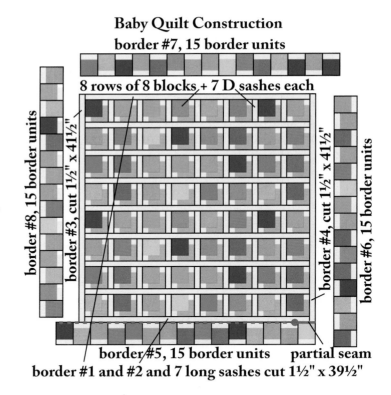

Baby Quilt Construction
border #7, 15 border units

border #8, 15 border units

border #3, cut 1½" x 41½"

8 rows of 8 blocks + 7 D sashes each

border #4, cut 1½" x 41½"

border #6, 15 border units

border #5, 15 border units partial seam

border #1 and #2 and 7 long sashes cut 1½" x 39½"

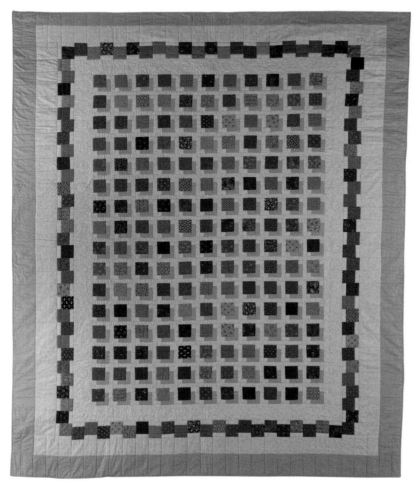

Another Look for Newport Beach

Designed by Judy Martin; pieced by Ardis Winters; quilted by Mary Hazelwood. Ardis substituted country colors for contemporary ones in the squares, shadows, and background. Her quilt varies in size from the ones in the book with a different number of blocks and two extra plain borders beyond the pieced border.

94

Father's Fancy

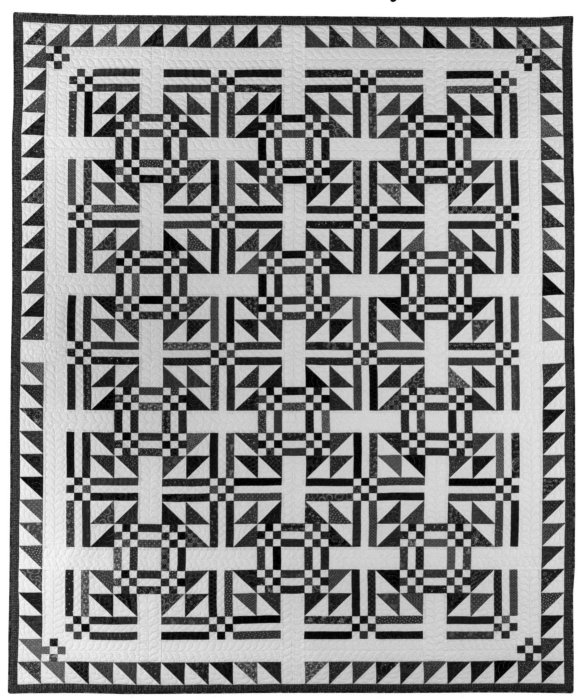

72" x 90" twin quilt designed and pieced by Judy Martin; quilted by Kathy Olson. I made this quilt for publication in Quilter's Newsletter Magazine *in 1993. It was inspired by a traditional Young Man's Fancy. I changed the design to make the cream of the traditional block appear to cross over the striped sashing. In fact, the cream is the sashing. I used a two-color plan of red scraps with an ivory solid. The reds are mostly calicoes. The scraps for this quilt were fairly uniform in color, but you could just as easily dance all around a color.*

Yardage, Dimensions, & Number of Blocks for Various Quilt Sizes

Yardage	Queen	Twin	Wall
Cream Solid **Red Prints** **Binding** **Backing**	6¼ yds./25 fat qtrs. 6¼ yds./25 fat qtrs. ¾ yd. 9⅛ yds.	5 yds./20 fat qtrs. 4½ yds./18 fat qtrs. ¾ yd. 5¾ yds.	2½ yds./10 fat qtrs. 1¾ yds./7 fat qtrs. ½ yd. 3⅝ yds.
Quilt Dimensions **Block Size** **Number of Blocks** **Set**	96" x 96" 15", 12" x 15", 12" 9 W, 12 X, 4 Y 5 x 5	72" x 90" 15", 12" x 15", 12" 6 W, 10 X, 4 Y 4 x 5	53" x 53" 15", 12" x 15", 12" 1 W, 4 X, 4 Y 3 x 3

 Cutting Requirements for Various Quilt Sizes

Fabric	Queen #18" Strips #borders	Queen #Patches border size	Twin #18" Strips #borders	Twin #Patches border size	Wall #18" Strips #borders	Wall #Patches border size
Cream Solid						
3⅞" x 3⅞"	38	300 B	30	240 B	14	108 B
3½" x 15½"	12	12 G	10	10 G	4	4 G
3½" x 9½"	48	48 F	39	39 F	20	20 F
3½" x 3½"	0*	20 A	0*	16 A	0*	8 A
1½" x 6½"	2*	80 E	0*	62 E	0*	24 E
1½" x 3½"	16	64 C	12	48 C	4	16 C
1½" x 1½"	43	465 D	33	360 D	14	145 D
Red Prints						
Borders		2 @ 5" x 96½" 2 @ 5" x 87½"		2 @ 2" x 87½" 2 @ 2" x 72½"		2 @ 1½" x 53½" 2 @ 1½" x 51½"
3⅞" x 3⅞"	38	300 B	30	240 B	14	108 B
1½" x 6½"	80	160 E	62	124 E	24	48 E
1½" x 3½"	32	128 C	24	96 C	8	32 C
1½" x 1½"	34	372 D	27	288 D	11	116 D
Binding		2" x 400"		2" x 340"		2" x 225"
Backing	3 panels @	35" x 104"	2 panels @	40" x 98"	2 panels @	31" x 61"

Cut out the F patches before cutting strips for A and E patches. You can cut all of the A patches from the strip ends left over from cutting F's. You can also cut each of the remaining F strip ends down to two 1½" strips and cut most of the E patches as well.

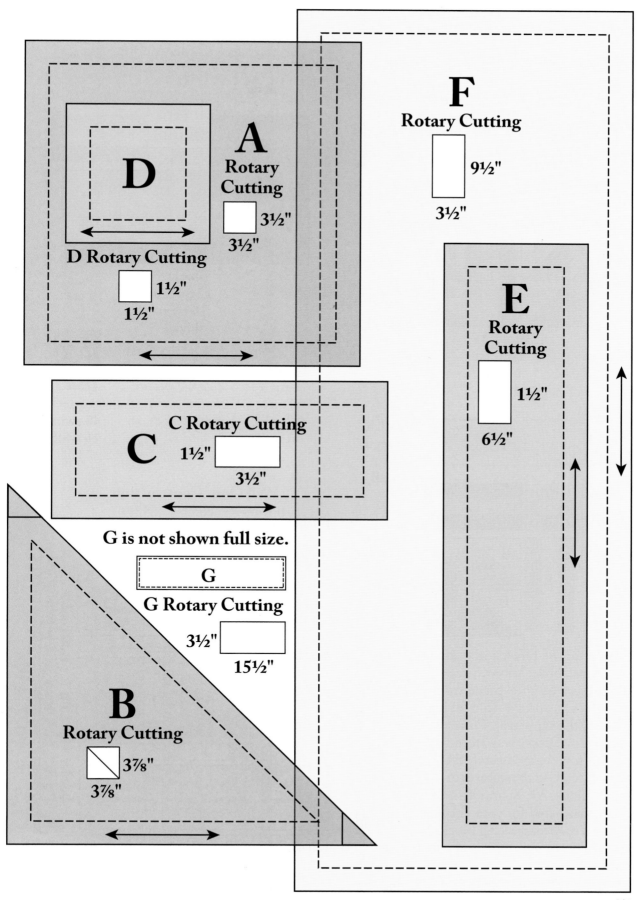

D

A
Rotary Cutting

3½"

3½"

D Rotary Cutting

1½"

1½"

F
Rotary Cutting

9½"

3½"

C

C Rotary Cutting

1½"

3½"

E
Rotary Cutting

1½"

6½"

G is not shown full size.

G

G Rotary Cutting

3½"

15½"

B
Rotary Cutting

3⅞"

3⅞"

Unit and Block Construction

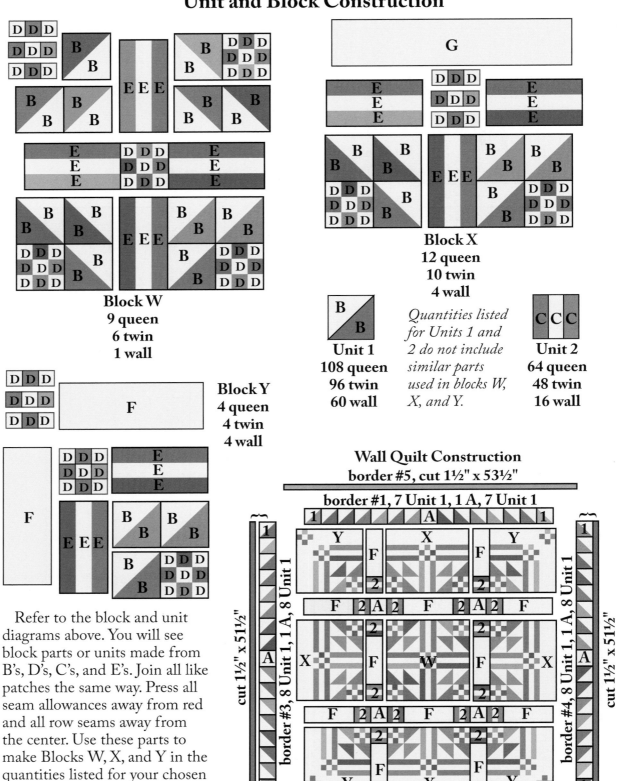

Block W
9 queen
6 twin
1 wall

Block Y
4 queen
4 twin
4 wall

Block X
12 queen
10 twin
4 wall

Unit 1
108 queen
96 twin
60 wall

Quantities listed for Units 1 and 2 do not include similar parts used in blocks W, X, and Y.

Unit 2
64 queen
48 twin
16 wall

Refer to the block and unit diagrams above. You will see block parts or units made from B's, D's, C's, and E's. Join all like patches the same way. Press all seam allowances away from red and all row seams away from the center. Use these parts to make Blocks W, X, and Y in the quantities listed for your chosen quilt size. After making blocks, you will have parts left over corresponding to the Units 1 and 2 needed for sashing and borders.

Wall Quilt Construction
border #5, cut 1½" x 53½"

border #1, 7 Unit 1, 1 A, 7 Unit 1

cut 1½" x 51½"
border #3, 8 Unit 1, 1 A, 8 Unit 1

cut 1½" x 51½"
border #4, 8 Unit 1, 1 A, 8 Unit 1

border #2, 7 Unit 1, 1 A, 7 Unit 1

border #6, cut 1½" x 53½"

Quilt Construction

Sew a single Unit 2 to each of the remaining F rectangles. Press the seams toward the red. Add a second Unit 2 to the opposite end of these until you run out of Unit 2's.

Lay out these X, Y, and F parts plus the W blocks and A patches as shown in the quilt construction diagram for your size. Join blocks and parts to make the wide block rows and narrow sash rows shown in the diagrams. Join the rows.

Join Unit 1's and the remaining A patches in the quantities listed in the quilt diagrams to make 4 borders. Attach the borders to the quilt in numerical order.

Queen Quilt Construction

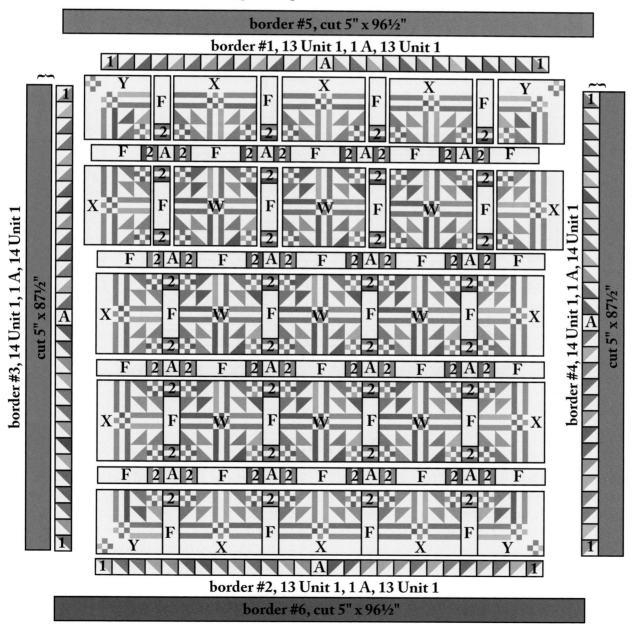

Twin Quilt Construction

border #5, cut 2" x 72½"

Quilt Finishing

Prewash and press the backing fabric. Trim off selvages and square up the fabric. Cut out backing panels in the size and quantity listed in the cutting chart. Pin and seam together the backing panels.

At this point, you may send out the top for quilting. If you will be hand or machine quilting it yourself, plan the quilting and mark it if necessary. Kathy Olson quilted in the ditch around the red and quilted simple feathers in the cream rectangles. Unless your quilting frame has rollers for batting and backing, you will need to baste the layers. To baste, lay the backing face down, and center the batting and the quilt top, face up, over it. Thread baste or pin baste with safety pins, trying to avoid the path of your planned quilting. Quilt, remove any markings, and bind to finish.

Grandma's Scrapbook

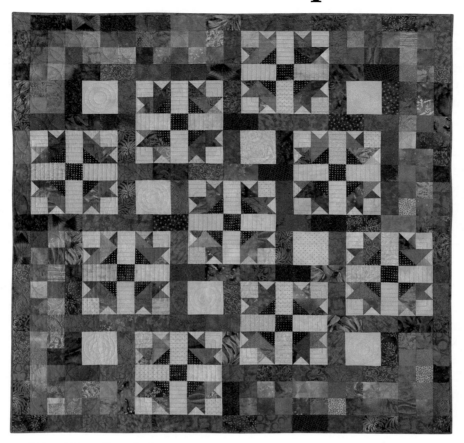

50" x 50" wall quilt designed and pieced by Judy Martin; quilted by Margy Sieck. Bright batik and contemporary-style scraps play off a sunny yellow scrap background and a single green batik accent fabric. I danced around pink, using everything from orange to red violet, with some pinks lighter than others. To contrast with the pinks, the purples lean toward the blue violet and are less variable. I used a "paint-by-number" quilt plan, with the yellows, pinks, purples, and green placed in the same patches in each block and unit.

I first published Grandma's Scrapbook as a block in 1998 in The Block Book. *That block was shown in multi-color '30s reproduction prints and unbleached solid, which would also suit this quilt. I devised this staggered arrangement especially for the block.*

Yardage and Dimensions for Various Quilt Sizes

Yardage	Queen/King	Twin	Wall
Purple Prints Pink/Orange Prints Yellow Prints Green Print Binding Backing	5 yds./20 fat qtrs. 4 yds./16 fat qtrs. 4¾ yds./19 fat qtrs. 1 yd. ¾ yd. 8¾ yds.	3½ yds./14 fat qtrs. 3 yds./12 fat qtrs. 3¼ yds./13 fat qtrs. ¾ yd. ¾ yd. 7¼ yds.	1½ yds./6 fat qtrs. 1¼ yd./5 fat qtrs. 1¼ yd./5 fat qtrs. ¼ yd. ½ yd. 3½ yds.
Quilt Dimensions "Block" Size	92" x 104" 10"	74" x 92" 10"	50" x 50" 10"

 **Cutting Requirements for Various Quilt Sizes**

Fabric	Queen/King		Twin		Wall	
	#18" Strips	#Patches	#18" Strips	#Patches	#18" Strips	#Patches
Purple Prints ▭ 2½" x 4½" □ 2½" x 2½"	 148 6	 442 B 32 A	 105 6	 313 B 34 A	 40 3	 120 B 16 A
Pinks/Oranges ⊠ 5¼" x 5¼" ⊠ 2⅞" x 2⅞" ⊠ 3¼" x 3¼" □ 2½" x 2½"	 15 18 18 37	 176 C 176 D 352 E 220 A	 10 12 12 32	 120 C 120 D 240 E 188 A	 3 4 4 19	 36 C 36 D 72 E 112 A
Yellow Prints □ 4½" x 4½" ⊠ 3¼" x 3¼" ▭ 2½" x 4½" □ 2½" x 2½"	 13 18 59 30	 39 F 352 E 176 B 176 A	 9 12 40 20	 26 F 240 E 120 B 120 A	 3 4 12 6	 8 F 72 E 36 B 36 A
Green Print ⊠ 2⅞" x 2⅞" □ 2½" x 2½"	 18 8	 176 D 44 A	 12 5	 120 D 30 A	 4 2	 36 D 9 A
Binding		2" x 405"		2" x 350"		2" x 215"
Backing	3 panels @	38" x 100"	3 panels @	34" x 82"	2 panels @	29¼" x 58"

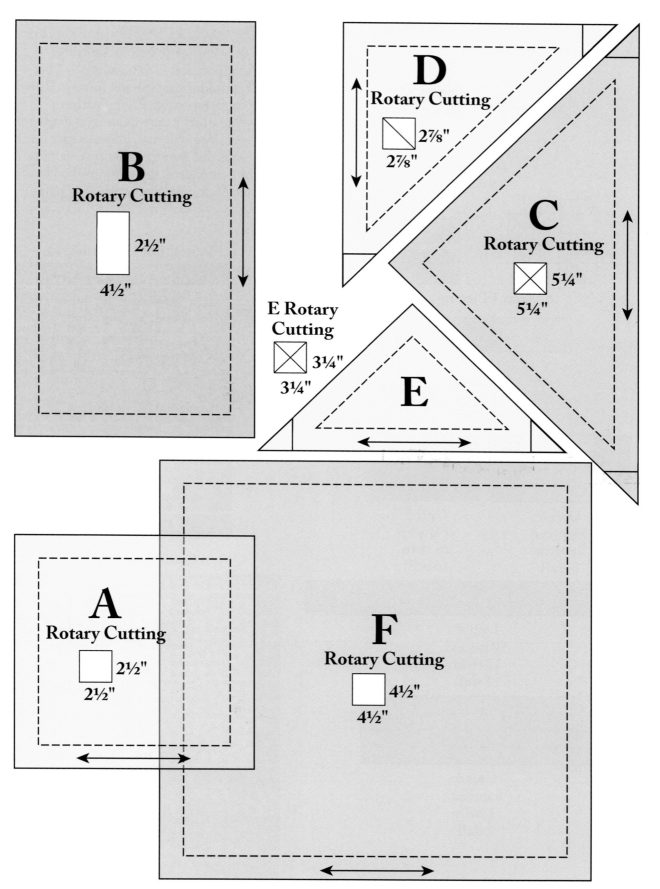

B
Rotary Cutting
2½"
4½"

D
Rotary Cutting
2⅞"
2⅞"

C
Rotary Cutting
5¼"
5¼"

E Rotary Cutting
3¼"
3¼"

E

A
Rotary Cutting
2½"
2½"

F
Rotary Cutting
4½"
4½"

Unit Construction

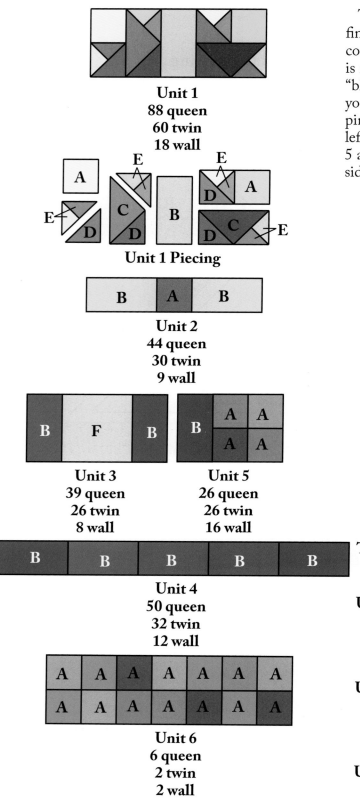

Though they appear to be blocks in the finished quilt, partial-block units are used to construct Grandma's Scrapbook in rows. There is no need to match scrap fabrics within a "block." Make units in the quantities listed for your quilt size. You will have some purple and pink A squares and some purple B rectangles left over for completing the sections. For Units 5 and 6, join A's in pairs before joining pairs side by side.

Unit 1
88 queen
60 twin
18 wall

Unit 1 Piecing

Unit 2
44 queen
30 twin
9 wall

Unit 3
39 queen
26 twin
8 wall

Unit 5
26 queen
26 twin
16 wall

Unit 4
50 queen
32 twin
12 wall

Unit 6
6 queen
2 twin
2 wall

Twin Quilt Construction

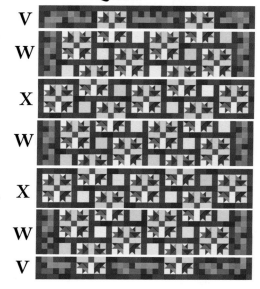

Queen Quilt Construction

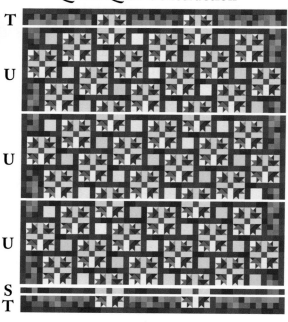

Quilt Construction

Join units and leftover A and B patches to make rows, then sections, in the quantities shown in the section diagrams. Join sections as shown in the quilt construction diagrams. Turn the V, T, or Y sections opposite directions at the top and bottom of the quilt.

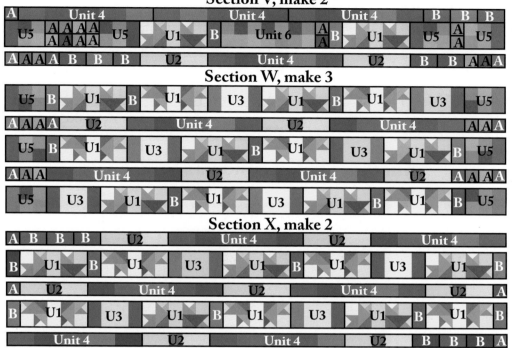

Twin Quilt Section Construction
Section V, make 2

Section W, make 3

Section X, make 2

Queen Quilt Section Construction
Section T, make 2

Section U, make 3

Section S, make 1

Quilt Finishing

Pin and seam together the backing panels. Layer and baste with thread or safety pins. Quilt and bind to finish.

Wall Quilt Construction

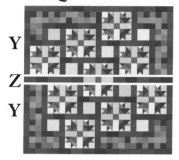

Y
Z
Y

Wall Quilt Section Construction
Section Y, make 2

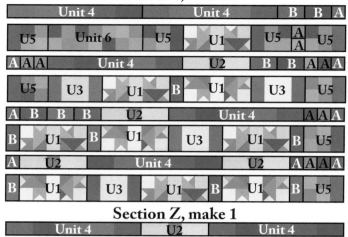

Unit 4			Unit 4			B	B	A
U5	Unit 6		U5	U1		U5	A / A	U5
A A A	Unit 4			U2		B B	A A A
U5	U3	U1	B	U1	U3		U5
A B B B	U2		Unit 4			A A A
B	U1	B	U1	U3	U1	B	U5
A	U2	Unit 4		U2	A A A
B	U1	U3	U1	B	U1	B	U5

Section Z, make 1

Unit 4	U2	Unit 4

Another Look: Grandma's Scrapbook

62" x 74" lap quilt or throw designed by Judy Martin; pieced by Sherry Folks; quilted by Mary Hazelwood. No pattern is given for this size. Country plaid homespuns in deep blues and greens provide an entirely different look for this variation. Sherry made her quilt with mixed dark blues and dark greens substituted for both the pinks and the purples of the pattern. She replaced yellow with tan and substituted light blue for the green. Sherry made the light blue patches match within the "block." This required planning the layout carefully because each "block" is made from 3 different units in 3 different rows of the quilt.

Fanfare for the Heroes

92" x 92" queen-sized quilt designed and pieced by Judy Martin; quilted by Sherry Rogers-Harrison. Bright batik and contemporary scraps form stars to contrast with pastel scrap stars in the background. 48 smaller stars join in to make this anything but the Lone Star that inspired it. Unlike a Lone Star, which is rarely a scrap quilt,

Fanfare for the Heroes utilizes scraps to add color nuances in a paint-by number plan. Bright blues range from royal and ultramarine to grape, with a variety of values, as well. Pinks include coral and orange. Greens extend to turquoise. Yellows vary less. (The difference between pastel and bright is not as great for yellow as it is for other hues.)

107

Yardage and Dimensions for Various Quilt Sizes

Yardage	Queen	Twin	Wall
Bright Blues	5½ yds./22 fat qtrs.	4½ yds./18 fat qtrs.	2 yds./8 fat qtrs.
Bright Yellows	1¼ yds./5 fat qtrs.	¾ yd./3 fat qtrs.	½ yd./2 fat qtrs.
Bright Green/Turq.	¾ yd./3 fat qtrs.	¾ yd./3 fat qtrs.	¾ yds./3 fat qtrs.
Bright Pinks	2¾ yds./11 fat qtrs.	1¾ yds./7 fat qtrs.	1 yd./4 fat qtrs.
Pale Blues/Greens	2¾ yds./11 fat qtrs.	2¾ yds./11 fat qtrs.	1¾ yds./7 fat qtrs.
Med. Pinks/Yellows	2½ yds./10 fat qtrs.	2½ yds./10 fat qtrs.	1½ yds./6 fat qtrs.
Binding	¾ yd.	¾ yd.	½ yd.
Backing	8¾ yds.	7⅜ yds.	4 yds.
Quilt Dimensions	92" x 92"	75" x 92"	62" x 62"

Cutting Requirements for Various Quilt Sizes

Fabric	Queen #18" Strips #borders	Queen #Patches border size	Twin #18" Strips # borders	Twin #Patches border size	Wall #18" Strips # borders	Wall #Patches border size
Bright Blues						
Border	–		–		4 @	2½" x 63¼"
⊠ 13¼" x 13¼"	–		1	4 G	–	
◹ 9⅜" x 9⅜"	14	28 F	14	28 F	–	
⊠ 6¼" x 6¼"	20	160 D	9	72 D	2	16 D
◹ 3⅜" x 3⅜"	21	208 C	11	104 C	4	32 C
⟋ 2" x 2"	37	184 A	37	184 A	37	184 A
Bright Yellows						
⟋ 2" x 2"	4	16 A	4	16 A	4	16 A
⟋ 1¾" x 1¾"	38	224 B	22	128 B	11	64 B
Bright Greens						
⊠ 6¼" x 6¼"	2	16 D	2	16 D	2	16 D
◹ 3⅜" x 3⅜"	4	32 C	4	32 C	4	32 C
⟍ 2" x 2"	7	32 A	7	32 A	7	32 A
Bright Pinks						
⟍ 2" x 2"	5	24 A	5	24 A	5	24 A
⟍ 1¾" x 1¾"	112	672 B	64	384 B	32	192 B
Pale Blues/Grn.						
⊠ 6¼" x 6¼"	14	112 D	14	112 D	6	48 D
◹ 5⅞" x 5⅞"	12	48 E	12	48 E	12	48 E
◹ 3⅜" x 3⅜"	8	72 C	8	72 C	–	

Cutting Requirements for Various Quilt Sizes, continued

Fabric	Queen		Twin		Wall	
	#18" Strips #borders	#Patches border size	#18" Strips # borders	#Patches border size	#18" Strips # borders	#Patches border size
Med. Pinks/Yel. 1¾" x 1¾"	102	608 B	102	608 B	54	320 B
Binding		2" x 385"		2" x 350"		2" x 265"
Backing	3 panels @	34" x 100"	3 panels @	34" x 83"	2 panels @	35½" x 70"

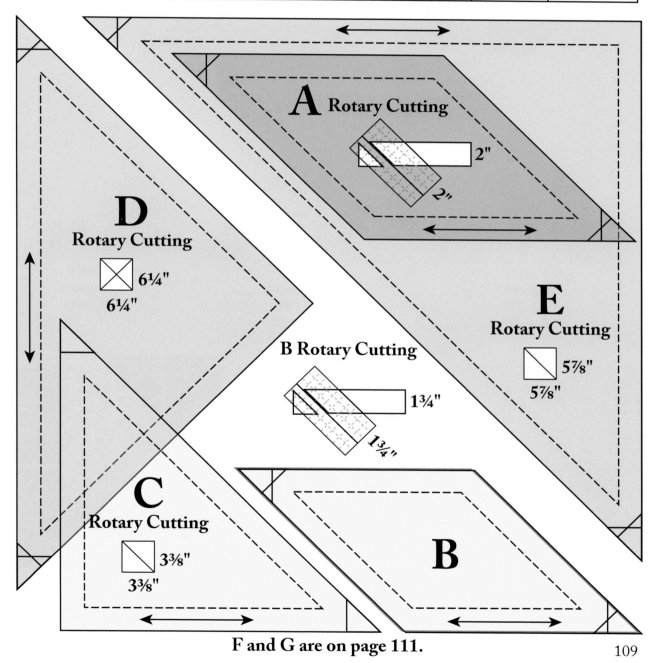

F and G are on page 111.

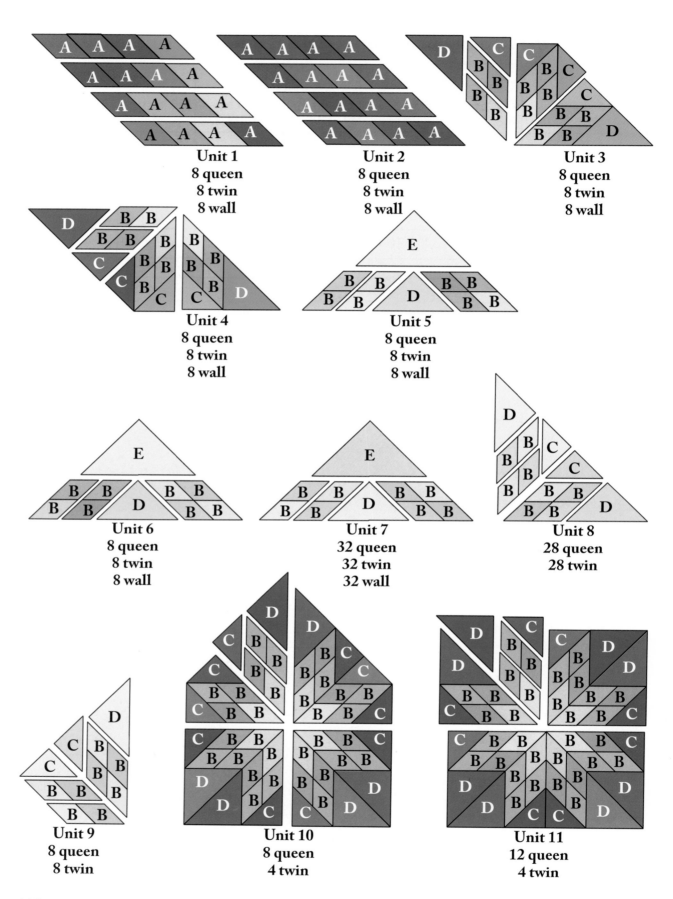

Unit 1
8 queen
8 twin
8 wall

Unit 2
8 queen
8 twin
8 wall

Unit 3
8 queen
8 twin
8 wall

Unit 4
8 queen
8 twin
8 wall

Unit 5
8 queen
8 twin
8 wall

Unit 6
8 queen
8 twin
8 wall

Unit 7
32 queen
32 twin
32 wall

Unit 8
28 queen
28 twin

Unit 9
8 queen
8 twin

Unit 10
8 queen
4 twin

Unit 11
12 queen
4 twin

110

Unit Construction

When you cut out the diamonds, be sure to trim all of the diamonds' points as shown in the templates to help you align them for stitching. Join blue, green, pink, and yellow A diamonds to make 8 Unit 1's. Finger press seams within a row away from the center of the star; press seams joining rows toward the center. Join remaining blue A's to make 8 Unit 2's, pressing as before.

Join 2 bright pink B diamonds; join 1 bright pink and 1 bright yellow B. Join pairs, with yellow at the point. Finger press seam allowances within rows away from the yellow point; finger press last seam toward the yellow. Make 64 of these diamond 4-patches.

Join four medium pink B's in a similar fashion to make a diamond 4-patch; make 152 for queen or twin; make 48 for the wall size.

Use the bright and medium diamond 4-patches, along with C, D, and E patches to make Units 3–11 in the quantities listed for your quilt size. Press seams away from the diamonds where possible.

Quilt Construction

Refer to the quilt construction diagram for your quilt size. Join Units 1–11 as shown to make a section of the quilt. For the queen and wall sizes, make 4 quarters; join to make 2 halves. Join halves. For the wall quilt, add borders and miter corners. For the twin, make two halves as shown in the diagram; join halves to complete the quilt. Press well.

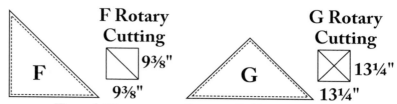

F Rotary Cutting 9⅜" 9⅜"

G Rotary Cutting 13¼" 13¼"

F and G are not shown full size.

Queen Quilt

¼ Queen Quilt Construction

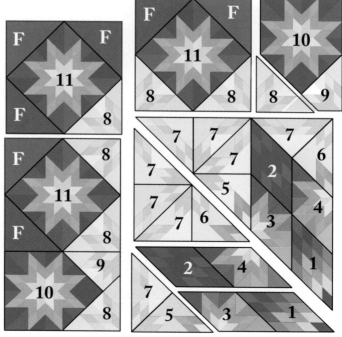

Wall Quilt

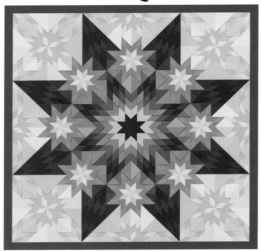

Finishing the Quilt

Seam the backing panels; press. Layer and baste backing, batting, and quilt top. Quilt as desired; bind to finish. Sherry Rogers-Harrison quilted Fanfare for the Heroes with scallops, rays, stripes, and freehand feathers.

Twin Quilt

¼ Wall Quilt Construction

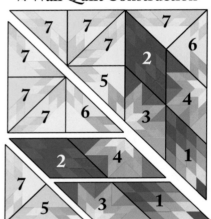

½ Twin Quilt Construction

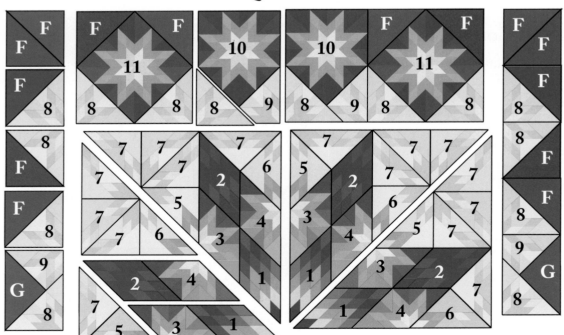

Ring of Fire

82⅛" x 97" twin quilt designed and pieced by Judy Martin; quilted by Kathy Olson. The quilt is named after the song. It always brings a smile to my face when my rock–and–roll husband plays recordings of Johnny Cash (and any of seventeen other artists) singing Ring of Fire. The quilt's toile background sets the style for this quilt. The tan and dark scraps have a 19th Century feel. Two background fabrics and the black border provide relief from the scrappy blocks. Gold scraps are fairly uniform. Darks include green, burgundy, black, and dark brown; all are similar in value.

113

Yardage and Dimensions for Various Quilt Sizes

Yardage	Queen	Twin	Wall
Black Print	2⅞ yds./10 fat qtrs.	2⅝ yds./10 fat qtrs.	1⅞ yds./4 fat qtrs.
Gold Prints	3½ yds./14 fat qtrs.	3⅝ yds./ 13 fat qtrs.	2½ yds./10 fat qtrs.
Dark Cream Print	1¾ yds./7 fat qtrs.	1¼ yds./5 fat qtrs.	¾ yd./3 fat qtrs.
Light Cream Print	3¼ yds./13 fat qtrs.	2¾ yds./11 fat qtrs.	1¼ yds./5 fat qtrs.
Various Darks	4¾ yds./19 fat qtrs.	4 yds./ 16 fat qtrs.	1¾ yds./7 fat qtrs.
Binding	¾ yd.	¾ yd.	½ yd.
Backing	9¼ yds.	8 yds.	4⅛ yds.
Quilt Dimensions	97" x 97"	82⅛" x 97"	61½" x 61½"
Block Size	10¼"	10¼"	10¼"
Number of Blocks	25 blocks set 5 x 5	20 blocks set 4 x 5	9 blocks set 3 x 3

Cutting Requirements for Various Quilt Sizes

Fabric	Queen #18" Strips #borders	Queen #Patches border size	Twin #18" Strips #borders	Twin #Patches border size	Wall #18" Strips #borders	Wall #Patches border size
Black Print						
Borders	2 @	5½" x 97½"	2 @	5½" x 87½"	2 @	2⅝" x 62"
	2 @	5½" x 87½"	2 @	5½" x 82⅝"	2 @	2⅝" x 57¾"
⊠ 3⅜" x 3⅜"	8	160 E	8	146 E	6	104 E
⧅ 1⅞+" x 1⅞+"	1	4 C	1	4 C	1	4 C
Gold Prints						
Borders	2 @	2⅜" x 81⅛"	2 @	2⅝" x 77⅜"	2 @	2⅞" x 51⅜"
	2 @	2⅜" x 77⅜"	2 @	2⅜" x 66¼"	2 @	2⅞" x 46⅝"
☐ 3+" x 8⅝"	16	16 N	14	14 N	8	8 N
☐ 3+" x 3+"	1	4 M	1	4 M	1	4 M
⊠ 3⅜" x 3⅜"	9	172 E	8	156 E	6	108 E
☐ 2" x 5⅝"	6	16 I	5	14 I	3	8 I
☐ 2" x 3+"	2	8 K	2	8 K	2	8 K
☐ 2" x 2⅝"	3	16 H	3	14 H	2	8 H
☐ 2" x 2"	25	200 F	23	177 F	15	116 F
⧅ 1⅞+" x 1⅞+"	3	44 C	3	40 C	2	28 C
☐ 1½+" x 2"	5	40 L	5	36 L	3	24 L
☐ 1½+" x 1½+"	20	200 D	16	160 D	8	72 D
Dark Cream Print						
☐ 5⅝" x 5⅝"	6	16 J	4	12 J	2	4 J
⊠ 3⅜" x 3⅜"	4	80 E	4	62 E	2	24 E
☐ 2" x 5⅝"	22	64 I	16	48 I	6	16 I
☐ 2" x 2⅝"	11	64 H	8	48 H	3	16 H

Cutting Requirements for Various Quilt Sizes, continued

Fabric	Queen		Twin		Wall	
	#18" Strips	#Patches	#18" Strips	#Patches	#18" Strips	#Patches
Light Cream Print ⊠ 5½" x 5½"	17	200 B	14	160 B	6	72 B
◇ 4¼" x 4¼"	7	100 G	5	80 G	3	36 G
◻ 2⅜" x 2⅜"	29	400 O	23	320 O	11	144 O
Various Darks ◸2⅝" x 3⅞"	50	200 A	40	160 A	18	72 A
◻ 2" x 2"	82	656 F	68	542 F	35	280 F
◻ 1⅞+" x 1⅞+"	25	400 C	20	320 C	9	144 C
Binding		2" x 410"		2" x 380"		2" x 260"
Backing	3 panels @	35½" x 105"	3 panels @	35½" x 90"	2 panels @	35" x 69½"

To rotary cut G, start by cutting a 4¼" square and cutting across it twice diagonally to make 4 triangles. For each of these triangles, lay both 2" lines of the ruler to align with the corner of the triangle as shown. Cut off both tips of the triangle where they extend beyond the ruler to complete G.

To rotary cut A, cut a rectangle 2⅝" x 3⅞". Cut off the upper right corner at a 45° angle as shown. (If you have a Shapemaker 45 ruler, you can conserve fabric by cutting a 2⅝" x 5⅛" rectangle, laying the 3⅞" line of the S45 on one end of it, and cutting along the angled end to make 2 A's.)

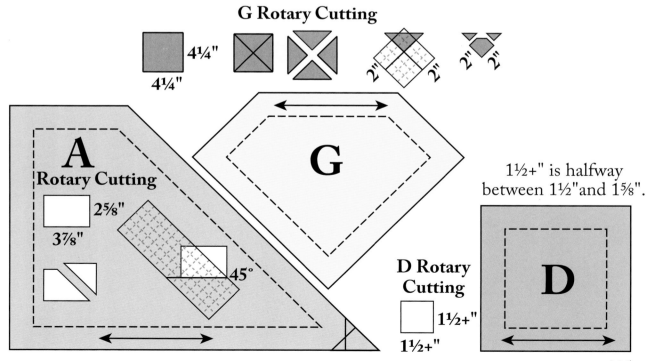

115

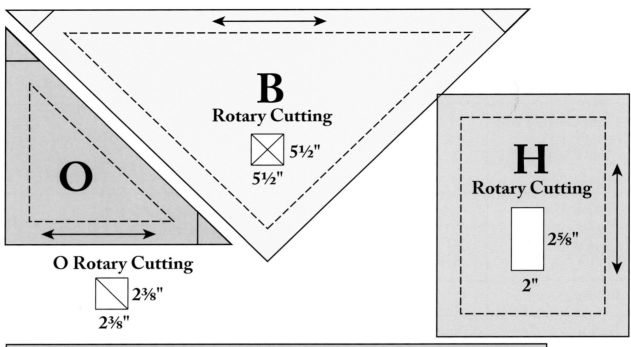

B
Rotary Cutting

5½"
5½"

O

O Rotary Cutting

2⅜"
2⅜"

H
Rotary Cutting

2⅝"
2"

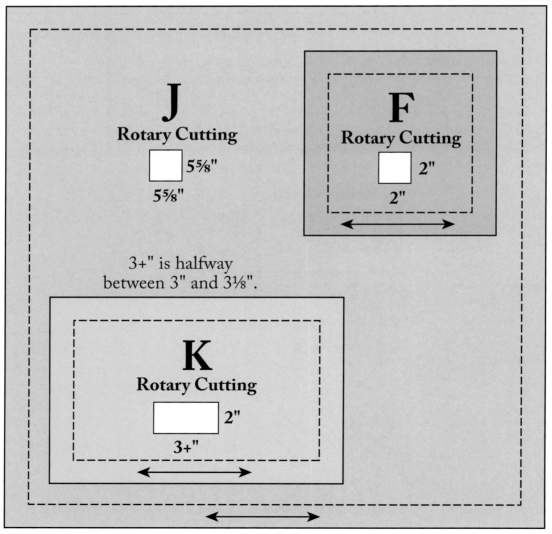

J
Rotary Cutting

5⅝"
5⅝"

F
Rotary Cutting

2"
2"

3+" is halfway
between 3" and 3⅛".

K
Rotary Cutting

2"
3+"

116

E Rotary Cutting

3⅜"
3⅜"

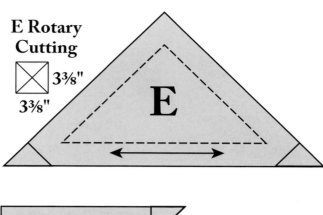

C Rotary Cutting

1⅞+"
1⅞+"

1⅞+" is halfway between 1⅞" and 2".

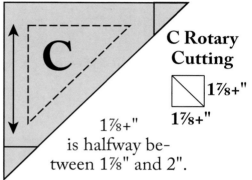

L Rotary Cutting

1½+"
2"

1½+" is halfway between 1½" and 1⅝".

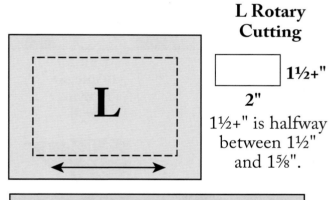

M Rotary Cutting

3+"
3+"

3+" is halfway between 3" and 3⅛".

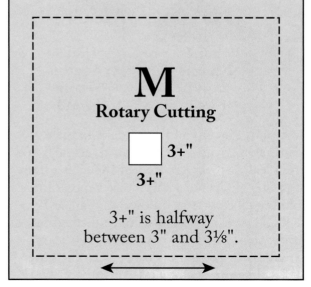

N Rotary Cutting

8⅝"
3+"

3+" is halfway between 3" and 3⅛".

I Rotary Cutting

5⅝"
2"

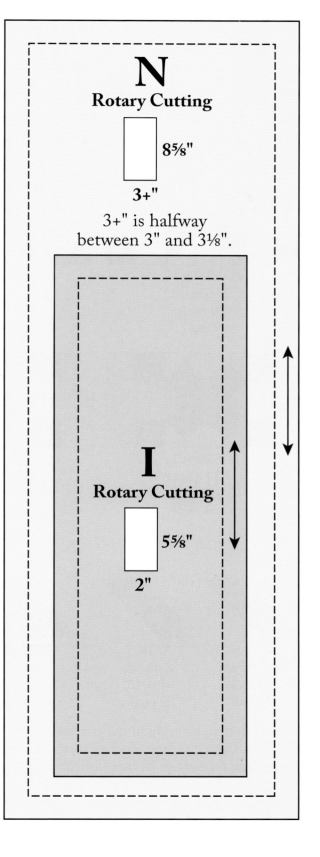

Block and Unit Construction

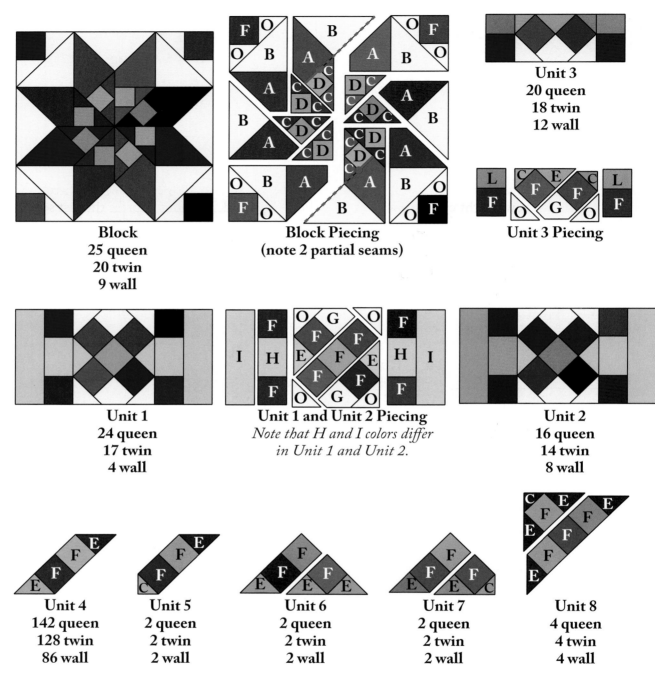

Block
25 queen
20 twin
9 wall

Block Piecing
(note 2 partial seams)

Unit 3
20 queen
18 twin
12 wall

Unit 3 Piecing

Unit 1
24 queen
17 twin
4 wall

Unit 1 and Unit 2 Piecing
*Note that H and I colors differ
in Unit 1 and Unit 2.*

Unit 2
16 queen
14 twin
8 wall

Unit 4
142 queen
128 twin
86 wall

Unit 5
2 queen
2 twin
2 wall

Unit 6
2 queen
2 twin
2 wall

Unit 7
2 queen
2 twin
2 wall

Unit 8
4 queen
4 twin
4 wall

Note that all pressing in these instructions refers to finger-pressing. To avoid stretching bias edges, do not use an iron until all bias edges have been stitched. Sew two matching C's to each gold D. Press seams away from D. Sew a light cream B to each A, as shown in the block diagram; press seams to oppose later seams. Arrange 8 of each of these to form a star, matching C scraps to A scraps to make

diamonds. Sew two O's to a dark F; press seams away from F. Stitch this to an A-B and press seams toward B. Repeat for each corner of the block. Make a half block, proceeding counter-clockwise as follows: Join an A-B to a C-C-D with a partial seam (indicated by a pink solid line in the diagram). The seam extends only from one end of D to the other and will be pressed toward A. Add a C-C-D,

118

pressing toward the first part. Add the matching corner piece; press toward the corner piece. Add the next C-C-D, then the matching A-B, pressing as before. Add one more C-C-D and its matching corner and press. Make another half the same way. Join halves. Complete the two partial seams. Make the number of blocks listed for your quilt size.

For Units 1 and 2, sew a dark F to each end of each dark cream H and each gold H; press seam allowances toward F's. Sew a gold I to the side of the ones with gold H's and a dark cream I to the ones with dark cream H's. Press seams toward I's. Sew a light cream G and a dark cream E to a dark F; add O. Repeat. Sew two dark F's to a gold F; add the F parts from the previous step to the sides. Attach two dark cream H parts to the dark cream E sides of the center to complete Unit 1 as shown. Make the listed number of Unit 1's. Unit 2 is made like Unit 1, except using one gold and one dark

cream H part. Make Unit 2's in the quantity listed for your chosen quilt size.

For Unit 3, sew a gold C and a gold E to a dark F. Sew a gold C and a light cream G to another F. Join these, and add two light cream O's as shown. Sew a dark F to each gold L. Sew one of these to each side of the part from the last step to complete Unit 3. Make these in the quantity listed for your quilt size.

Referring to the diagrams, make Units 4–8 in the quantities listed. Press seam allowances toward dark F's and black E's. For Units 6 and 7, press the last seam of each unit away from the F-F-E end. For Unit 8, press the last seam toward corner with the black C.

Join Unit 4's to make 4 border strips, finger-pressing seam allowances all to one side. Sew Unit 6 to one end of two of these pieced border strips, as shown. Sew Unit 5 to one end and Unit 7 to the other end of the two remaining pieced border strips.

Wall Quilt Construction

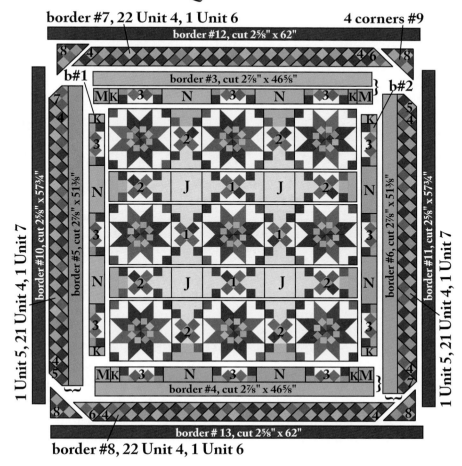

border #7, 22 Unit 4, 1 Unit 6   **4 corners #9**

border #8, 22 Unit 4, 1 Unit 6

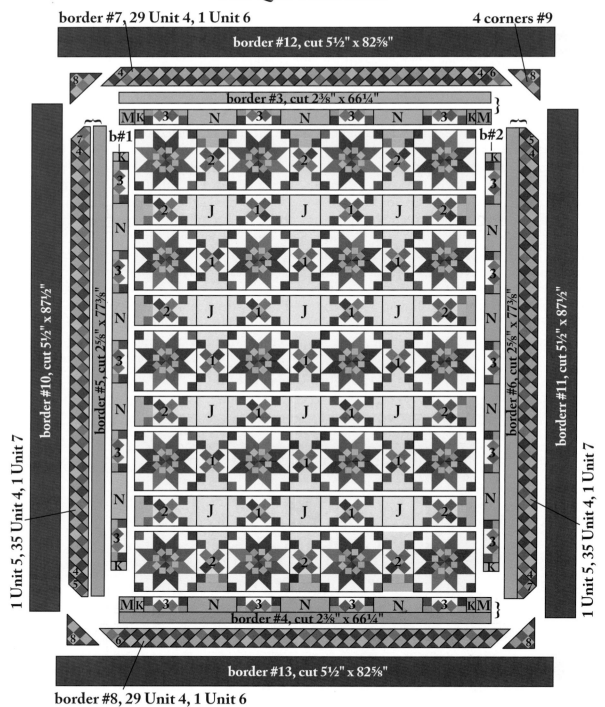

border #7, 29 Unit 4, 1 Unit 6

4 corners #9

border #12, cut 5½" x 82⅝"

border #3, cut 2⅜" x 66¼"

border #10, cut 5½" x 87½"

border #5, cut 2⅝" x 77⅜"

border #6, cut 2⅝" x 77⅜"

borderr #11, cut 5½" x 87½"

1 Unit 5, 35 Unit 4, 1 Unit 7

1 Unit 5, 35 Unit 4, 1 Unit 7

border #4, cut 2⅜" x 66¼"

border #13, cut 5½" x 82⅝"

border #8, 29 Unit 4, 1 Unit 6

Quilt Construction

Referring to the quilt diagram, arrange blocks, Unit 1's, Unit 2's, and dark cream J squares as shown. Join blocks and units to make wide rows, pressing seam allowances away from the blocks. Join units and J's to make narrow rows, pressing toward the units. Join rows. Join K, M, and N patches and Unit 3's. Attach these and gold borders. Pin and stitch the pieced borders to the quilt. Add Unit 8's. Finally, add the black borders.

border #9, 36 Unit 4, 1 Unit 6

4 corners #11

border #14, cut 5½" x 97½"

border #5, cut 2⅜" x 81⅛"

b#1

border #7, 1 Unit 5, 35 Unit 4, 1 Unit 7

border #12, cut 5½" x 87½"

border #3, cut 2⅜" x 77⅜"

border #4, cut 2⅜" x 77⅜"

border #13, cut 5½" x 87½"

border #8, 1 Unit 5, 35 Unit 4, 1 Unit 7

b#2

border #6, cut 2⅜" x 81⅛"

border #15, cut 5½" x 97½"

border #10, 36 Unit 4, 1 Unit 6

Quilt Finishing

Trim off selvages and square up the backing fabric. Cut panels as listed in the cutting chart. Pin and seam together the backing panels.

For my Ring of Fire, Kathy Olson quilted in the ditch around stars and squares; she quilted feathers in the toile and borders.

After you mark the quilting, baste the layers together as follows: Lay the backing face down, and center the batting and the quilt top, face up, over it. Thread baste or pin baste with safety pins, trying to avoid the path of your planned quilting. Quilt and bind to finish.

The Spanish Steps

70" x 85" twin quilt designed and pieced by Judy Martin; quilted by Pam Clarke. Traditional prints featuring lush florals as well as small motifs include country scraps as well as reproduction 19th Century scraps. I started with a color scheme of olive, gold, tan, black, teal, brick, and grape. The quilt is made in a block-by-block plan, with each W block using just one dark fabric. A single fabric is used for background. The border is more or less randomly scrappy.

Chains of squares appear to float and cast shadows over the light background. This effect is most easily achieved with just one background fabric and one shadow fabric. The shadow fabric should be somewhat darker, duller, and less detailed than the background fabric.

Yardage and Dimensions for Various Quilt Sizes

Yardage	Queen	Twin	Wall
Lt. Cream Print Dark Cream Print Various Darks Binding Backing	5½ yds. 1½ yds. 5¼ yds./21 fat qtrs. ¾ yd. 8⅝ yds.	4¾ yds. 1 yd. 3½ yds./14 fat qtrs. ¾ yd. 6⅞ yds.	2¼ yds. ½ yd. 2 yds./8 fat qtrs. ½ yd. 3⅝ yds.
Quilt Dimensions Block Size	90" x 90" 7½"	70" x 85" 7½"	52½" x 52½" 7½"

Cutting Requirements for Various Quilt Sizes

Fabric	Queen #18" Strips #borders	Queen #Patches border size	Twin #18" Strips #borders	Twin #Patches border size	Wall #18" Strips #borders	Wall #Patches border size
Light Cream						
Borders	1 @	4¼" x 69¼"	1 @	4¼" x 69¼"	1 @	3" x 43"
Borders	1 @	3" x 69¼"	1 @	3" x 69¼"	1 @	1¾" x 43"
Borders	1 @	4¼" x 75½"	1 @	4¼" x 60½"	1 @	3" x 39¼"
Borders	1 @	3" x 75½"	1 @	3" x 60½"	1 @	1¾" x 39¼"
6¾" x 8"	4	8 E	4	7 E	2	4 E
6¾" x 6¾"	16	32 D	12	24 D	4	8 D
1¾" x 8"	4	8 F	4	7 F	2	4 F
1¾" x 3"	33	164 C	26	128 C	11	52 C
1¾" x 1¾"	32	288 B	25	225 B	11	92 B
Dark Cream						
1¾" x 3"	19	91 C	15	72 C	7	31 C
1¾" x 1¾"	36	319 B	28	248 B	11	99 B
Various Darks						
3" x 3"	121	601 A	79	392 A	44	217 A
Binding		2" x 375"		2" x 325"		2" x 225"
Backing	3 panels @	33¼" x 98"	3 panels @	29" x 78"	2 panels @	31" x 61"

In the block-by-block coloring that I used, just one dark fabric appears in each block. In order to accomplish this, you will need to cut A squares in matched sets. Matching is easy to do for The Spanish Steps because one 17-18"strip yields the five A squares needed for one W block. Matching occurs naturally when you use fat quarters.

Unit Construction

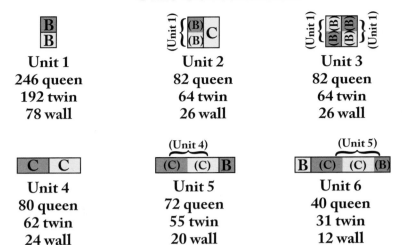

Unit 1
246 queen
192 twin
78 wall

Unit 2
82 queen
64 twin
26 wall

Unit 3
82 queen
64 twin
26 wall

Unit 4
80 queen
62 twin
24 wall

Unit 5
72 queen
55 twin
20 wall

Unit 6
40 queen
31 twin
12 wall

Unit 1. Join a dark cream B square to a light cream B. Press seam allowances toward the darker B. Make the listed quantity.

Unit 2. Add a light cream C rectangle to one of the Unit 1's already made to make a Unit 2. Make the number listed.

Unit 3. Join the remaining Unit 1's (already made) in pairs as shown to make 4-patches. Press seams to one side.

Unit 4. Set aside 9 (queen), 8 (twin) or 5 (wall) dark cream C's and one fewer light cream C for borders #1 and #2. Join the remaining C's in dark cream-light cream pairs, stitching along one short side. Press seam allowances toward the darker C.

Unit 5. Sew a dark cream B to one of the Unit 4's already made. Press seams toward dark. Make the listed number of Unit 5's.

Unit 6. Sew a light cream B to the C end of one of the Unit 5's already made. Press seams toward dark. Make the listed number of Unit 6's. You should have 1 dark and 2 light cream B's and 3 dark and 2 light cream C's left for the borders.

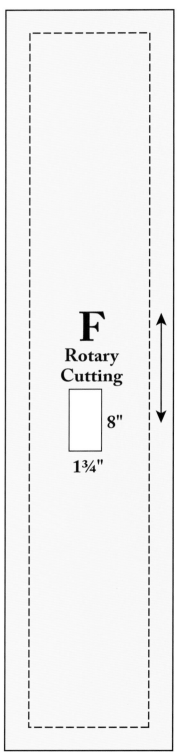

F
Rotary Cutting

8"

1¾"

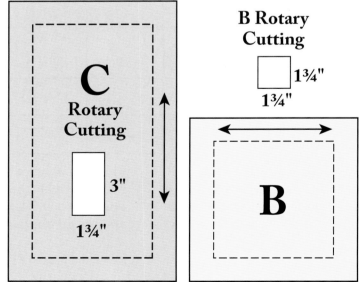

C
Rotary Cutting

3"

1¾"

B Rotary Cutting

1¾"

1¾"

B

Block Construction

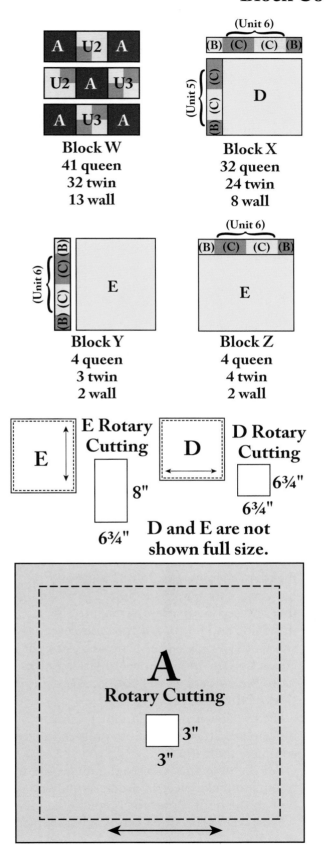

Block W
41 queen
32 twin
13 wall

Block X
32 queen
24 twin
8 wall

Block Y
4 queen
3 twin
2 wall

Block Z
4 queen
4 twin
2 wall

E Rotary Cutting
8"
6¾"

D Rotary Cutting
6¾"
6¾"

D and E are not shown full size.

A Rotary Cutting
3"
3"

Block W. Choose five matching A squares. Join these with 2 Unit 2's and 2 Unit 3's to make three rows as shown. Press seam allowances toward A's. Join rows. Press seams to one side to complete block W. Make the quantity listed for your quilt size.

Block X. Sew one Unit 5 to each D; press seams away from D. Add one Unit 6 to each D segment to complete X block; press seam allowances toward D.

Block Y. Sew one Unit 6 to the long side of E as shown to make a Y block . Press seams toward E. Make the listed number of Y's.

Block Z. Notice that Y and Z blocks are made from the same pieces with Unit 6's turned differently. For Z, sew the opposite side of Unit 6 to E's long side. Press seams toward E. Make the listed number of Z blocks.

Border Unit Construction

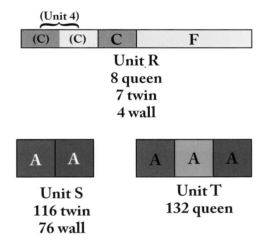

Unit R
8 queen
7 twin
4 wall

Unit S
116 twin
76 wall

Unit T
132 queen

Unit R. Sew a dark cream C to each remaining Unit 4; add F to one end. Press seams toward the darker cream. This completes the R units. Make them in the listed quantity.

Unit S (twin and wall only). Choose two dark A patches from different fabrics. Join them to make Unit S. Press seams to one side. Make the number required for your quilt size.

Unit T (queen only). Choose three dark A patches of different fabrics. Join them to make Unit T. Press seams to one side. Make 132 T units for the queen-sized quilt.

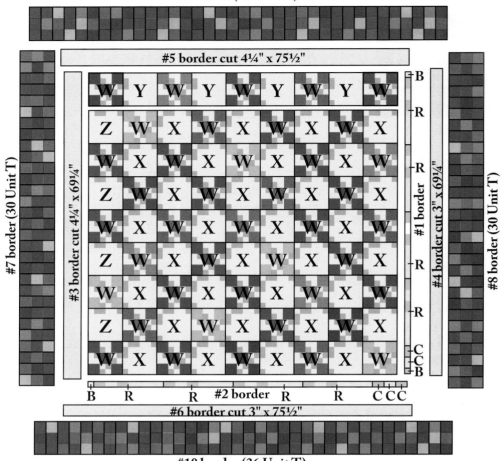

Queen Quilt Construction
#9 border (36 Unit T)

#5 border cut 4¼" x 75½"

#7 border (30 Unit T)

#3 border cut 4¼" x 69¼"

#1 border

#4 border cut 3" x 69¼"

#8 border (30 Unit T)

W	Y	W	Y	W	Y	W	Y	W
Z	W	X	W	X	W	X	W	X
W	X	W	X	W	X	W	X	W
Z	W	X	W	X	W	X	W	X
W	X	W	X	W	X	W	X	W
Z	W	X	W	X	W	X	W	X
W	X	W	X	W	X	W	X	W
Z	W	X	W	X	W	X	W	X
W	X	W	X	W	X	W	X	W

B R R R R C C B

B R R #2 border R R C C C

#6 border cut 3" x 75½"

#10 border (36 Unit T)
Add borders in numerical order.

Wall Quilt Construction
#9 border (21 Unit S)

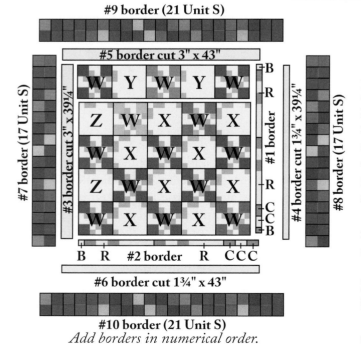

#5 border cut 3" x 43"

#7 border (17 Unit S)

#3 border cut 3" x 39¼"

#1 border

#4 border cut 1¾" x 39¼"

#8 border (17 Unit S)

W	Y	W	Y	W
Z	W	X	W	X
W	X	W	X	W
Z	W	X	W	X
W	X	W	X	W

B R R C C B

B R #2 border R C C C

#6 border cut 1¾" x 43"

#10 border (21 Unit S)
Add borders in numerical order.

Quilt Construction

Join W, X, Y, and Z blocks as shown to make rows. Join rows. Join R units and light and dark patches B and C to make first and second borders. Attach to the right side and bottom of the quilt center as shown to complete the shadows. Add light cream borders in numerical order, with the narrower borders on the bottom and right sides of the quilt.

For the queen size quilt, join T units to make pieced borders. Add to quilt center to complete quilt top.

For the twin and wall sized quilts, join S units to make pieced borders as shown. Sew to the quilt center to complete the top.

Press well. Trim thread ends and pick off stray threads.

Twin Quilt Construction

#9 border (28 Unit S)

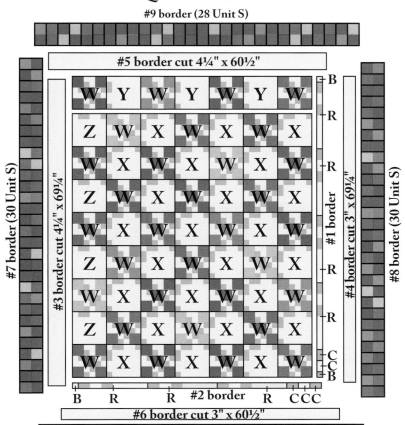

#5 border cut 4¼" x 60½"

#7 border (30 Unit S)

#3 border cut 4¼" x 69¼"

#1 border

#4 border cut 3" x 69¼"

#8 border (30 Unit S)

W	Y	W	Y	W	Y	W
Z	W	X	W	X	W	X
W	X	W	X	W	X	W
Z	W	X	W	X	W	X
W	X	W	X	W	X	W
Z	W	X	W	X	W	X
W	X	W	X	W	X	W
Z	W	X	W	X	W	X
W	X	W	X	W	X	W

B
R
R
R
R
R
C
C
B

B R R **#2 border** R CCC

#6 border cut 3" x 60½"

#10 border (28 Unit S)

Quilt Finishing

Trim off the selvages, and square up the backing fabric. Cut out backing panels in the size and quantity listed in the cutting chart. Pin and seam together the backing panels.

Plan the quilting and mark it if necessary. Pam Clarke machine quilted in the ditch around the dark squares and quilted a simple curved motif and gridwork in the background. I recommend treating the shadows as part of the background to make them appear more like shadows and less like objects.

Lay the backing face down, and center the batting and the quilt top, face up, over it. Thread baste or pin baste with safety pins, trying to avoid the path of your planned quilting.

Quilt, remove any markings, and bind to finish.

Another Look for The Spanish Steps

90" x 90" queen quilt designed by Judy Martin; pieced and quilted by Margy Sieck. A wide variety of red prints from traditional to contemporary form the chains in this variation. A toile enlivens the background, and a small red-and-white check forms the shadows. The yardage and cutting can be easily adapted: simply substitute red prints for darks, toile for light cream, and red check for dark cream.

Other Judy Martin Books & Products

Stellar Quilts, 2010, 128 pages. 13 outstanding star quilts, each in 3 sizes. Enjoy the extra setting plans for three quilts and extra coloring ideas for many. Judy's new method makes easy work of rotary cutting unusual shapes without measuring. It's like using a rotary cutting template, but without the expense! Close-up color photos show every detail of the gorgeous quilting and yummy fabric choices. Quilts range from a simple Ohio star set in an intriguing Log Cabin variation to an exquisite Flying Swallows variation that gives the illusion of overlapping diamonds. Variable Stars are set in circles or ovals in one quilt. In another, LeMoyne stars embellish a simplified Double Wedding Ring. In one of the easier quilts Judy fashions stars from rectangles. In one of the masterpiece quilts, Judy combines two kinds of stars related to the Mariner's Compass.

Judy Martin's Log Cabin Quilt Book, 2007, 128 pages. 16 scrappy quilts from easy to masterpiece are presented with glorious color photographs and accurate patterns in multiple sizes. Close-up photos show the quilting and fabric in every detail. Lots of color diagrams show every part of making the quilts, from blocks, colors, piecing sequence, pressing, and borders to whole quilts. Genuinely original ideas add freshness to this classic pattern. Judy tweaks the patterns to suggest stars or curves. And the cutting and sewing involve simply squares and rectangles in almost every case. "The quilts in your new book look even more exciting than I've come to anticipate from you! Your extraordinary sense of color and style makes it fun to look at the book and dream of what I want to make next. Moreover, your reputation for providing accurate, thorough instructions makes the sewing as much fun and stress-free as the dreaming. Thanks for giving the quilt world such great new variations of the Log Cabin pattern. You've outdone yourself once again!" – Connie Doern, Creekside Quilting, Clive, Iowa

Piece 'n' Play Quilts, 2002, 96 pages. Choose from 12 new and easy Drunkard's Paths, stars, Log Cabins, Rail Fences, and more. Complete patterns with rotary cutting layouts and optional templates. It couldn't be simpler: First you follow the pattern and piece the blocks. Then you play with their arrangement until you find the look you want. You'll have creative independence with NO math! "I love the book. The hardest part is choosing which quilt to make first." – Sue M., Triangle, NY

Cookies 'n' Quilts, 2001, 80 pages. 8 original and complete quilt patterns feature interesting combina-

tions such as stars within stars, Maple Leafs combined with Log Cabins, and Virginia Reels made all from Logs. The cookies and bars are guaranteed to take your baking to a new level of delicious decadence. "Now, imagine this scenario: You are nestled all snug under your newly made quilt, and there's a plate filled with a variety of delicious cookies at your side... hmmm... I think you're going to l-o-v-e this book." – Joyce Libal, *Miniature Quilts*

The Creative Pattern Book, 2000, 176 pages. This book has it all – 27 complete quilt patterns (12 quilts and 15 wonderful variations) plus ideas for taking each pattern further. Find out what Judy was thinking when she designed the quilt. Learn all her secrets for dealing with bias, partial seams, handling fabric, and so much more! "*The Creative Pattern Book* is the best quilt book I own, period. Some books have good designs; some have good writing. Yours stand alone for quality of inspiration, clarity, and technique." – Gloria J., Crandon, WI

Judy Martin's Ultimate Rotary Cutting Reference, 1997, 80 pages. You'll find charts and instructions for cutting 52 shapes in countless sizes, plus detailed information on tools and techniques. Don't rotary cut again without the *Ultimate Rotary Cutting Reference!* "*Judy Martin's Ultimate Rotary Cutting Reference* is like a bible to a quilter. It is a must have. Everything is laid out for you. Since I am somewhat 'math-impaired,' the book has been very helpful." – Kay D., Longboat Key, FL

Point Trimmer, 1996. The Point Trimmer is the easiest way to pre-trim points, helping you align neighboring patches and reducing bulk in your quilt. "I don't know how anyone can sew without trimming the points. I just cannot believe what a difference it made in my piecing!! What a wonderful tool the Point Trimmer is! When I sewed the first two trimmed patches together, and they just fell into place, I could have cried for joy!" – Darlene W., Canfield, OH

Shapemaker 45, 1996. Save time, fabric, and money with the S45! Now you can easily rotary cut your favorite shapes – octagons, trapezoids, prisms, bow ties, house shapes, and much more. You'll cut shapes faster, with fewer strokes and no fabric waste. That will save you time, fabric & money! "I just converted a very old template pattern into rotary cutting using your very-easy-to-use instructions and the Shapemaker 45. Thank you so much for all your wonderful designs and tools." – Karen M., Littleton, CO

CROSLEY-GRIFFITH PUBLISHING COMPANY, INC. • www.judymartin.com • (800) 642-5615